THE NORMAN INVASION OF IRELAND

Richard Roche

D0062880

ANVIL BOOKS LIMITED

First published 1970 by
Anvil Books
45 Palmerston Road, Dublin 6
Reprinted 1979

This new edition 1995

4 6 8 9 7 5 3

ISBN 0 947962 81 6

Cover design Terry Myler
Typesetting by Computertype Limited
Printed by Colour Books Limited

'THE NORMANS and their Flemish and Welsh comrades had embarked at Milford Haven, their horses prancing aboard the ships, the shouts of command and farewell in French, Flemish and Welsh echoing across the water. Pennants fluttered from the long lances of the knights and the sunlight glinted on armour and shield.'

Thus, in the early days of May 1169, began 'the most far-reaching event that occurred in Ireland since the introduction of Christianity'.

Those first invaders – Robert FitzStephen, Robert and Meiler FitzHenry, Maurice de Prendergast, Harvey de Monte Marisco, Maurice Fitzgerald, Robert de Barri, Raymond le Gros and Strongbow – nearly all related by blood or marriage, were not seeking to conquer Ireland for the English Crown. They were freelance adventurers in search of land and booty, either by force or through marriage. They had little to lose in leaving Wales, everything to gain in Ireland …

The Norman Invasion of Ireland is a fascinating and eminently readable account of those momentous years, an account that begins in the Ireland of pre-invasion days, with its social structure and the intertribal warfare which led to the power struggle in which Dermot MacMurrough became involved – with such dire consequences. It traces the origins of the Normans, records the events that culminated in the landings at Bannow, Baginbun and Passage, and ends with the coming of Henry II and his takeover from Strongbow and the Geraldines.

Cover: The seal of Strongbow

1 *Tomb slab, Jerpoint Abbey*

To the proud people of
Forth and Bargy,
descendants of knights and barons

2 Norman knight, Jerpoint Abbey

3 A motte-and-bailey castle

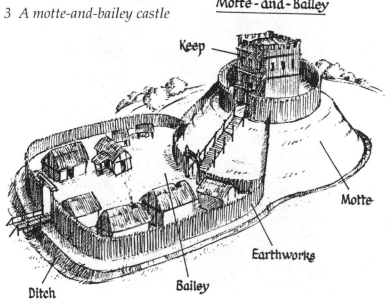

Motte - and - Bailey

Keep

Motte

Earthworks

Bailey

Ditch

Contents

Illustrations

Author's Preface

This book on the Norman invasion of Ireland started out as a labour of love on the origin of my own Norman-Flemish ancestors. As my research led me deep into the drama of those times and as fascination grew I was tempted to commit to paper many facts, hitherto unknown to me, about the invasion and those who took part in it.

I also was struck by the fact, as I consulted authority after authority, that there did not appear to be any handy-sized book available in which the story of the invasion and the invaders was told in a simple, straightforward manner. There are, to be sure, several contemporary or near-contemporary accounts but they are long out of print. There are also many learned histories of the era but in them the Norman invasion of Ireland is either dealt with in episodic fashion or treated briefly and generally in the context of European history or medieval times.

It is in an endeavour to fill this gap with a compact book that I have compiled this history. It is, in effect, a synthesis of many accounts and viewpoints but out of it, I hope, there emerges a fairly clear-limned picture of the circumstances that led to the invasion, of the actual landings and of the men and women who took part in those historical events.

While the facts of the story are the ancient chroniclers', the judgments generally are my own. If these do not at all times conform with the views of the authorities on the subject I hope the murmurs of dissent will not dissuade other readers from sharing in the drama and excitement of some of the most eventful years in the history of Ireland.

Richard Roche,
Duncormick,
County Wexford.

4 *A Norman ship*

Foreword

The Norman invasion of Ireland during the twelfth century is considered by most eminent historians to have been one of the most important events in the entire history of Ireland.

It has, in fact, been equated with the advent of Christianity to this country, in its long-term effects and far-reaching repercussions.[1] Things were never the same again following the arrival of the mail-clad invaders. With the dubious wisdom of over eight and a quarter centuries' hindsight we can now say that the most serious after-effect of the invasion was the resultant involvement of England in Irish affairs. Yet it should be realised that this was not the fault of the first invaders but rather the consequence of fear on the part of England's rulers that a rival Norman dynasty might be set up in Ireland.

Indeed at an early stage it looked as if Strongbow and his sturdy barons were about to do just that – until Henry II arrived and thwarted their unscheduled plans. How different the subsequent history of Ireland might have been had such a Norman state then been founded is now merely a subject for an exercise in imagination, but it can hardly have been as damaging to Ireland's interests as the English involvement in our affairs which has persisted down to the present day.

I will go as far as to say that the nation which probably would have evolved from an unrestricted Norman-Irish alliance would have been a successful one. As it was, by the time Norman and Irish had coalesced, England's grip on the country could not be loosened, even though valiant attempts to do so were made by the Irish and their Norman allies.

What we must bear constantly in mind, then, is that the first invaders of the years 1167, 1169, 1170 and 1171 did not come as England's official vanguard for total conquest but rather as freelance adventurers seeking a new home, and a new allegiance perhaps, beyond the reach of the king of England. Many of them were no longer in favour with Henry II; neither were they wanted by the Welsh whose lands they had appropriated.

They had little to lose in leaving Wales – they had everything to gain in Ireland, as Dermot MacMurrough made certain to let them know. So they came, they saw – and for a time looked like conquering.

Two factors, however, militated against their complete success: one was the anxiety and jealousy of King Henry and subsequent kings of England lest a rival Norman state be set up in Ireland; the other was the strange capacity of the Irish to survive defeat after defeat and finally to absorb the Normans into the national fabric when they became, as the old dictum describes, 'more Irish than the Irish themselves'.

The loose, tribal structure of Irish society at the time, which rendered the numerous tribes incapable of effective, unified resistance to an invader, was paradoxically the very failing which probably saved the Irish from total defeat.

'There was no massed national army to destroy, leaving the entire country at the mercy of the invader. There was no capital city, the capture of which would mark the downfall of the native government.'[2]

1

Sources

I am not so much concerned in this book with the after-effects of the Norman invasion as with the invasion itself, how it came about and how it was carried through. Our school history-books tell us little about the men who took part, sketching them as bold, bad marauders slaying the hapless Irish and filching their lands. More adult works are preoccupied with assessments and interpretations and give little attention to the personalities – both Norman and Irish – involved. Yet the men who make history are surely more fascinating than the history itself. But, one may ask, where can we now find the kind of personal detail which would bring those dead men to life? Strangely, for an event so far back in history, the Norman invasion of Ireland was unusually well chronicled. More important still, there are extant contemporary accounts drawing on actual eyewitness descriptions of the happenings and personalities of those days. It is on these that my narrative is based.

Probably the best-known of these twelfth-century chroniclers is Giraldus Cambrensis, Gerald the Welshman, whose two works on Ireland – *Topographia Hiberniae* (The Topography of Ireland) and *Expugnatio Hibernica* (The Conquest of Ireland) – have been the cause of controversy almost since the day they were first published.

Gerald was born about 1147 at Manorbier Castle in Pembrokeshire in Wales. His father was a Norman nobleman, William de Barri, and his mother Angharad was the daughter of Gerald de Windsor and his wife, the

15

5 Manorbier Castle

famous Nesta, who has been called 'the Helen of Wales' and who was the daughter of Rhys ap Tewdwr Mawr, the last independent prince of south Wales.

Gerald was therefore born to romance and adventure ... No doubt he heard, though he makes but sparing allusion to them, of the loves and adventures of his grandmother, the Princess Nesta. The daughter and sister of a prince, the wife of an adventurer, the concubine of a king and the paramour of every daring lover, a Welshwoman whose passions embroiled all Wales, and England too, in war, and the mother of heroes – FitzGeralds, FitzStephens and FitzHenrys and others – who, regardless of their mother's eccentricity in the choice of their fathers, united like brothers in the most adventurous undertaking of that age, the conquest of Ireland.[1]

Gerald de Barri, educated in Paris (where he also lectured), was a cleric who became archdeacon of Brecon in 1175, when he was only twenty-eight years of age. In the following year, on the death of his uncle, Bishop David FitzGerald of St David's, he was nominated together with the other archdeacons of the diocese for the choice of King Henry II as to who would be the new bishop of St David's.

Gerald, whose Welsh patriotism and detestation of the promotion of Normans to Welsh sees were well known, was, however, passed over. As a sop Henry soon afterwards made him a court chaplain. He paid his first visit to Ireland in 1183, partly, as he tells us in his *Expugnatio Hibernica*, to join in the Norman conquest, partly to see and explore the country and to examine 'the primitive origin of its race'. It may have been at this time that he visited his uncle Robert FitzStephen in Munster. In his role as court chaplain Gerald, in 1185, was commissioned by the king to accompany Prince John, lately created 'Lord of Ireland', to this country. He lived in Dublin for two years, making occasional excursions into those parts of the country colonised by his Cambro-Norman kinsmen, and it was during these two periods in 1183 and 1185-87 that he collected the materials for his *Topographia* and *Expugnatio*.

About Gerald's subsequent career we need not concern ourselves here, beyond noting that in 1188 he accompanied Archbishop Baldwin through Wales preaching the Third Crusade and presented the ageing archbishop with a copy of *Topographia* to read between sermons. He must, therefore, have completed it during the year after his return from Dublin.

Ten years later he failed again in a bid for the bishopric of St David's. There followed his long and historic fight for the see, in the course of which he visited Rome three times to plead his case before the pope. On one of these visits, in an effort to win the favour of Innocent III, Gerald

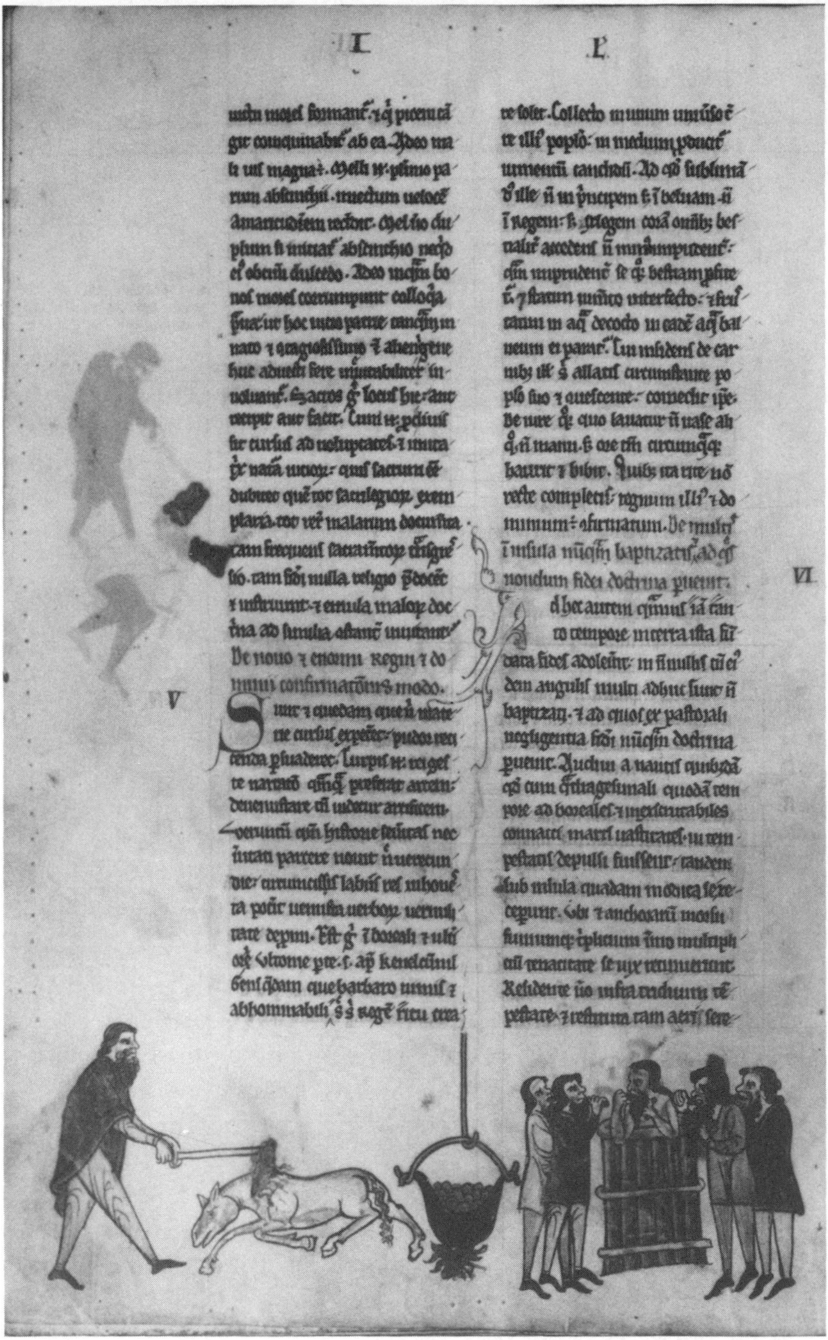

6 *Giraldus,* Topographia Hiberniae

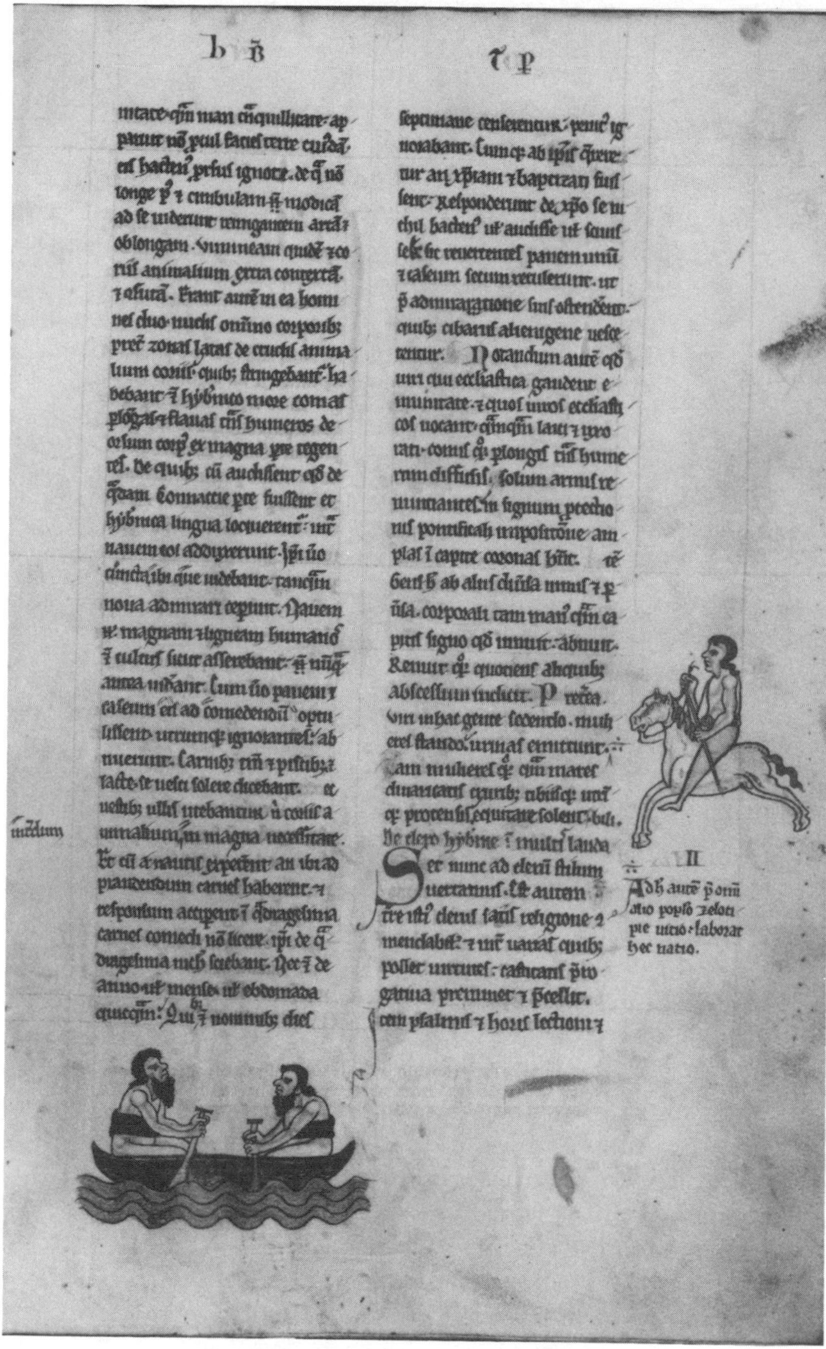

7 *Giraldus,* Topographia Hiberniae

presented him with six volumes of his work. Among them, perhaps, was his story of the conquest of Ireland. Failing in yet another attempt to attain the see of St David's in 1214, Gerald later withdrew from an active life, resigning his archdeaconry and prebend stall, making a final pilgrimage to Rome and then retiring to Lincoln to complete his literary labours. He died about 1223.

At this stage it would be well to assess Gerald's talents and accomplishments as a scholar and writer – and his failings as an historian – as we shall be depending considerably on his narrative about the Norman invasion hereafter.

He is widely acknowledged to have been a clever, cultured man, proud of his Welsh rather than his Norman origins. 'One of the most learned men of a learned age,' was how Professor Freeman, who edited his works, describes him. 'The cleverest critic of the life of his time,' was the verdict of another.[2]

He was apparently multi-lingual, writing in Latin and quoting extensively in Welsh, English, French, German, Hebrew, Greek and Irish. In at least four of these languages he was, it is said, fluent.

Probably the best summing-up on Gerald as a scholar and writer has been given by Kate Norgate:

> Gerald's wide range of subjects is only less remarkable than the ease and freedom with which he treats them. Whatever he touches – history, archaeology, geography, natural science, politics, the social life and thought of the day, the physical peculiarities of Ireland and the manners and customs of its people, the picturesque scenery and traditions of his own native land, the scandals of the court and the cloister, the petty struggle for the primacy of Wales, and the great tragedy of the fall of the Angevin Empire – is all alike dealt with in the bold, dashing, offhand style of a modern newspaper or magazine article. His first important work,

The Topography of Ireland, is, with due allowance for the difference between the tastes of the twelfth century and those of the nineteenth, just such a series of sketches as a special correspondent in our own day might send from some newly colonised island in the Pacific to satisfy or whet the curiosity of his readers at home.[3]

When it came to writing about Ireland, however, Gerald displayed unusual prejudice and rancour. This might have been understandable in one committed to a partisan stand in the struggle between Irish and Norman, but when such failings are combined with much downright inaccuracy it is not surprising that his works on Ireland have become suspect in the eyes of most historians.

As early as 1662, an Irish scholar, John Lynch, bishop of Killala, felt compelled to refute some of Gerald's statements, mainly those in *Topographia*. Dr Lynch entitled his work *Cambrensis Refuted*, and a sub-title read: 'Or rather historic credit in the affairs of Ireland taken from Giraldus Cambrensis who is proved to abound in most of the blemishes while destitute of most of the qualifications of a legitimate historian.'[4] In this work Dr Lynch certainly proved that Gerald 'abounded in blemishes' as an historian and geographer.

Another Irish nobleman and scholar of the times, one Philip O'Sullivan, refers to the 'enormous lies' of Gerald about Ireland.[5]

Gerald undoubtedly was inclined towards intellectual snobbery and credulity, and, like many a sensational writer since then, either did not bother or had not the opportunity to check his 'facts' before publishing. His account of the invasion of Ireland, dedicated to King John and 'the men of St David's' eulogises the invaders, his own kinsmen, at the expense of the 'mere Irish'. For all his skill with the pen – and his 'popular style' (his own phrase) is most readable and entertaining – Gerald

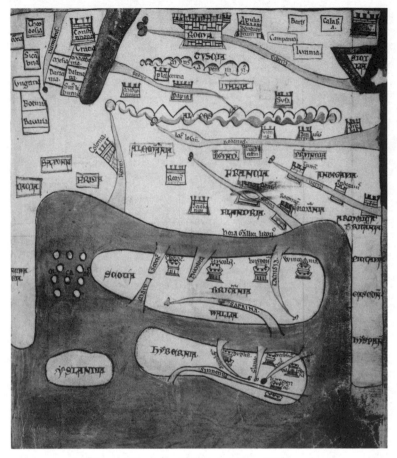

8 Map of Europe, Topographia Hiberniae

remains one to watch carefully in his descriptions of
Ireland and the Irish.

Yet his remains one of two contemporary accounts of
the Norman invasion on which we must fall back for most
of what we know about that event. Its prime value lies in
the fact that, although Gerald himself probably did not
witness the invasion or the preparations for it, he got from
his kinsmen among the invaders first-hand accounts of
what took place.[6]

He is probably exercising poetic licence when he writes (in his First Preface to *Expugnatio*) of 'transactions which have taken place under my own observation, of the greatest part of which I have been an eyewitness, and which are so fresh in my memory that I cannot have any doubt about them'.

As far as we know Gerald was in Paris, studying and lecturing, at the time of the invasion and did not return to Wales until 1172. It is possible he may have returned to Pembroke on holiday during the years 1166 to 1171 when the prelude to invasion and the actual incursions were being effected.

In the main, however, we must accept that most of his account derives from the statements and recollections of others: his brother Robert, for example, who was with the first party ashore at Bannow; his favourite cousin Raymond 'le Gros', whom he probably visited at the latter's castle near Tullow in 1185; his uncle Robert FitzStephen, or his other relatives and friends among the first invaders.

Therein lies the value of Gerald's narrative – no other writer had such splendid opportunities to gather these first-hand accounts of the invasion from the actual participants.

A last word on Gerald from Goddard Orpen may not be out of place here since it gives another opinion on this unusual man:

Owing to his (Gerald's) connexion with the invaders and to his inevitable want of sympathy with the Irish, it has been the fashion to discredit his statements and to represent his judgement as hopelessly warped ... He has even been charged with the deliberate forgery of important historical documents ... That his sympathies were with the invaders, and in particular with those of his relatives who took a leading part in the invasion, should of course always be carefully borne in mind, but a study of his writings has led me to regard him as an extraordinarily acute observer, and one who for his time was not peculiarly credulous, but also as a writer who (allowance being made for certain obvious pre-possessions) faithfully recorded what he saw and heard.[7]

The second contemporary source upon which we can draw for an eyewitness account of the invasion is not as well known as Gerald's *Expugnatio Hibernica*. It is a long, epic poem written in Old French called *Le Chansun de Dermot e li Quens* (The Song of Dermot and the Earl).[8]

The author of this strange work is unknown, although there is reason to believe that he may have been a Norman and a monk or scholar, and possibly resident in Ireland, at least for a time. *The Song* has often been attributed – wrongly – to Morice Regan, Dermot Mac-Murrough's 'latimer' or secretary, who was at the Wexford king's side throughout most of those eventful years and who acted as Dermot's ambassador and courier on several occasions. Early references in the poem itself disprove this, but the identity of the author has been the subject of dispute for many years.

Goddard Orpen, who edited and footnoted a translation of *The Song* has this to say of its authorship:

> There was ... an Irishman who was a participator in the events, and though his account has not come down to us at first hand, there is every reason to believe that it is faithfully retailed to us by the writer of the Old French rhymes contained in this volume. This Irishman was Morice Regan ... and he was no doubt an eyewitness of much that the Anglo-Norman rhymer tells on his authority.[9]

Orpen also claims that it is possible to put an approximate date on the poem:

> As to the date of the poem we have first of all the statement that our author met Morice Regan in the

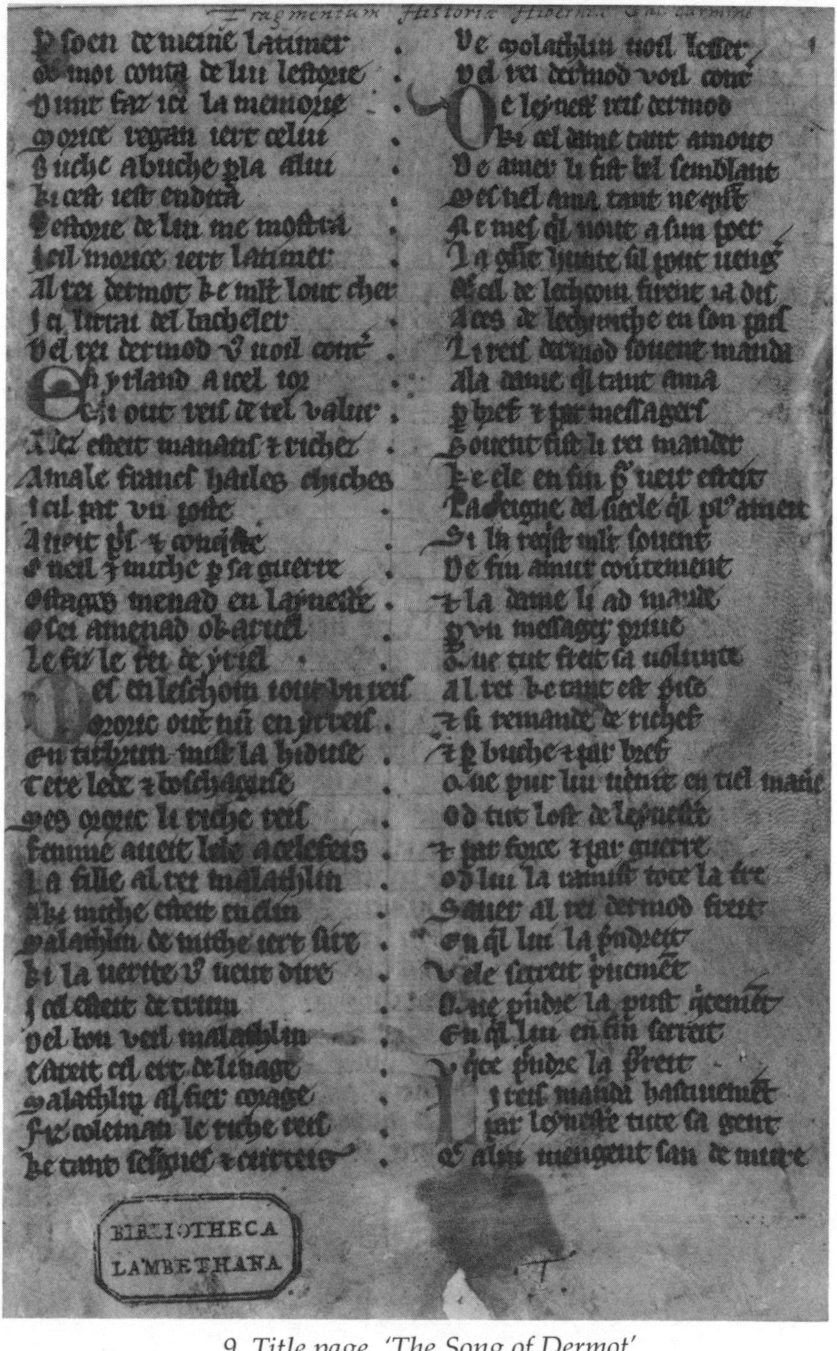

9 *Title page, 'The Song of Dermot'*

Le Chansun de Dermot
The Song of Dermot

Par soen demeine latimer	By his personal interpreter
Que moi conta de lui l'estorie	Who told me the story about him
Dunt faz ici la memorie.	Of which I make a record here.
Morice Regan iert celui,	Morice Regan was that man,
Buche a buche parla a lui	Mouth to mouth he spoke to him
Ki cest jest endita:	Who composed this narrative:
L'estorie du lui me mostra.	He showed me the story about him
Icil Morice iert latimer	That Morice was interpreter
Al rei Dermot, ke mult l'out cher.	To King Dermot, who loved him dearly.
Ici lirrai del bacheler,	Here I shall leave aside the retainer,
Del rei Dermod vus voil conter.	I want to tell you about King Dermot.

En Yrland, a icel jor,	In Ireland, at that time
N'i out reis de tel valur:	There was no king of suchlike valour:
Asez esteit manans e richez,	Very powerful and rich was he
Ama le francs, haï les chiches.	He loved the generous, he hated the mean.
Icil par un [soen] posté	He by his own might
Aveit pris et conquesté	Had taken and conquered
O'Neil e Mithe par sa guerre,	O'Neill and Meath in his war;
Ostages menad en Laynestere:	He took hostages back to Leinster:
O sei amenad O'Karuel,	He took with him O'Carroll,
Le fiz le rei de Yriel.	The son of the king of Uriel.

flesh, and as the latter was employed on an important embassy to Wales in 1168, and was sent to summon Dublin to surrender in 1170, we can hardly place his birth later than about 1147. Supposing he was eighty years of age when he told the story to the writer we get 1227 as an outside date. Looking at the contents of the chronicle we find that the narrative is brought regularly down in the fragment only to 1175 or 1176, but there are two allusions pointing to a much later date.

From another allusion we cannot place the composition of the poem, in its present form at least, earlier than the beginning of the thirteenth century ... we cannot place its date very long after 1225.[10]

Orpen suggests that there may have been a pre-existing version, written probably soon after Strongbow's death in 1176, and there are references in the poem to an existing 'lay' or 'song'.

These theories, however, have been disputed by J. F. O'Doherty, who holds that *The Song* was actually composed by the person who writes therein in the first person and that this writer had been in communication with the 'bachelor's secretary' mentioned in the opening lines.[11] This 'bachelor's secretary', often confused with Morice Regan, apparently was in possession (if not actually the author) of a rhymed chronicle and the composer of this rhymed chronicle in turn had been in touch with Regan.

O'Doherty dates *The Song* later than 1225, if not 1231, fifty years after the events it describes and says that:

... its value as a source for the history of the Anglo-Norman invasion of Ireland must be called seriously in question ... It cannot be used as a standard with which to judge the accuracy of plain prosaic records such as those contained in the bold statements of the native annals, or in the fuller and more enthusiastic writings of Giraldus Cambrensis; but must rather itself be tested by these other accounts of the invasion.

Whoever the author of *The Song of Dermot* was and whatever its date, it still remains one of the few near-contemporary accounts extant of the invasion. If its historical
accuracy is doubtful it is invaluable in other ways – in its
location of events such as battles and meetings and its
richness in relevant detail about those stirring and
colourful times.

There are, of course, gaps in the narrative, where
sections of the manuscript are missing or mouldered, but
sufficient remains to tell a coherent story. The poem is
very long and repetitious, employing the storyteller's
trick now and then of repeating lines or couplets to fix the
listener's attention anew on what is to come (or perhaps
to mark rest points in its narration). Like Gerald's account
it, too, is kind to the invaders and to Dermot, whom it
describes as 'noble king' or 'Dermot the renowned'.
Dermot's enemies are nowhere lauded, while the
Norsemen and Irish of Wexford town are called 'traitors'.
From such internal evidence it is safe to deduce that the
scribe was probably a Norman who came to Ireland in the
train of the invaders.

Against these two pro-Norman accounts have we any
Irish chronicles which can be used to level the balance?
The nearest thing to a contemporary native work is the
Book of Leinster, which was compiled under Dermot Mac-
Murrough's patronage and which was probably the chief
treasure of his library. Containing one of the most valuable collections of Celtic lore which have survived to the
present day, the *Book of Leinster* was largely compiled (or
perhaps transcribed) in the first half of the twelfth century
by Finn MacGorman, bishop of Kildare, who was honoured in his time as 'Chief Historian of Leinster' and who
died in 1160. The compilation was done by order of Aodh
MacCrimhthainn, Dermot's tutor, who was abbot of
Terryglass, County Tipperary.

This work, while providing much information about
pre-Norman Ireland, particularly about Leinster and its

kings and chief families, is of little or no value, however, as far as the actual Norman invasion is concerned. Its usefulness lies in the information which it supplies about the power struggle in Ireland before the invasion and in the pedigrees and pen-pictures of men like Dermot MacMurrough which it contains.

The contents of the *Book of Leinster* are also contained in the *Book of Lecan* and the *Book of Ballymote*. Most of the *Book of Leinster* is preserved in the library of Trinity College, Dublin, and the remainder, a smaller part, in the library of the Franciscan monastery, Dun Mhuire, Killiney, County Dublin.

By far the most fruitful, though by no means the most reliable, Irish source is the famed *Annals of the Four Masters*, compiled by the O'Clerys, a learned family who were hereditary historians to the O'Donnells, princes of Tir Conaill, now County Donegal. Three of the O'Clerys – Michael, Peregrine and Conary of Kilbarron, near Ballyshannon – and Peregrine O'Duigenan of Kilronan in County Roscommon were the chief compilers and they laboured many years before the work was completed in 1636.

The *Annals* were transcribed from older manuscripts, among them the *Annals of Tighernach*, the *Annals of Inisfallen*, the *Annals of Ulster*, the *Book of Conquests* and others. Starting at the earliest period of Irish history the *Annals of the Four Masters* bring us up to 1616 and thus, as one might expect, contain considerable information on the Norman invasion.

The unreliability of much of this information, however, arises primarily from the fact that it is, at best, third-hand, based on material originally written down centuries earlier from the recollections of others and inevitably suffering in the retelling and rewriting all the aberrations of faulty memory and partisan pen. Secondly, in its final transcription the information underwent another process which, laudable though it may have seemed to the

10 Irish scribe

transcribers, left the end result 'sicklied o'er' with pious patriotism.

Thus, while much of the source-material in the *Annals of the Four Masters* is undoubtedly contemporary and undeniably useful, we must view it with a jaundiced eye and constantly remind ourselves that it is probably the labour of a holy man of Ireland intent on perpetuating the image of an island of saints and scholars.

Ironically, much the same kind of propagandist endeavour must have impelled Gerald de Barri to pen his eulogies of the invaders who also, we must remember, believed they were acting in the best interests of the same religion as that practised by the well-intentioned scribes of the various annals.

This leaves us, it may seem, with a rather one-sided view of the invasion, but we do have the benefits of hindsight and of the matured judgments of many later historians. Of such judgments and of the accounts of other annalists and chroniclers we shall be availing ourselves as we go along, annotating and elaborating on these sources in our progress.

2
Bridgeheads

Two parts of Ireland, those which we now call Antrim and Wexford, have for obvious geographical reasons been used as bridgeheads by incursors from earliest times. The seas between these parts and the sister isle of Britain were narrower and consequently were traversed by mariners and colonisers almost from the time man first settled in the islands of western Europe.

Wexford presents itself as a natural gateway to the rest of Ireland to any voyager approaching the coast from France or Wales. It is no surprise, therefore, to find that the Picts, who preceded the Celts to Ireland, spread into this country from Scotland and, via Wexford, from Wales.

O'Curry says it is recorded that the Picts fled from oppression in Thrace, passed into France (where they founded the city of Pictiers or Poictiers – the Poitiers which will figure later in our story) and, again being threatened, fled further to Britain and thence to Ireland, landing on the coast of Wexford.[1]

Crimthaun Sciath-Bel was at this period chief of this part of the country and at the time of the landing of the Picts was engaged in extirpating a tribe of Britons who had earlier settled in the forests of Fotharta (now the barony of Forth in south Wexford).

Gabriel O'C. Redmond believes that these Britons were probably driven by Crimthaun into what is now the Barony of Shelburne and from their descendants the area was designated Siol-Brannach.[2]

An earlier Wexford historian, Philip H. Hore, took a

31

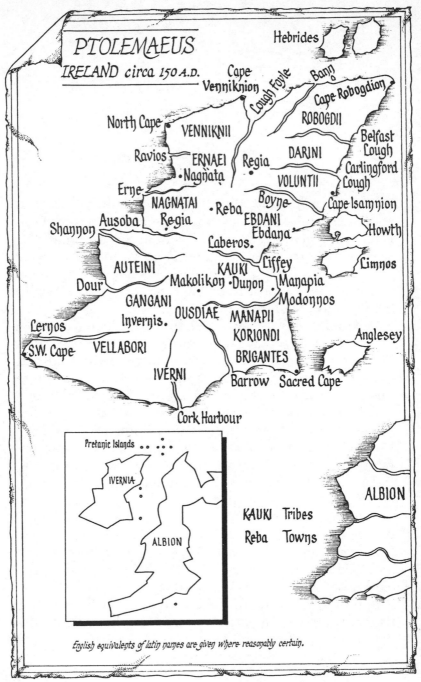

11 Ptolemy's map of Ireland

similar view: 'The Barony of Shelburne derives its name from having belonged in prehistoric times to the Siol-Brannach (seed or race of Britons), a colony apparently from the adjacent coast of Wales.'[3]

Succeeding waves of newcomers almost certainly used Wexford as their first landing-place. The Celts, who moved out of central Europe about 350 BC, into southern France and northern Spain, thence to Brittany, Britain and Ireland, probably first set foot in Ireland on the beaches of Wexford. The Menapii, Celts from the area now known as Flanders, gave their name to Menapia, the cognomen used by map-maker Ptolemy to pin-point the place now called Wexford.

It was through Wexford that Christianity first spread – from Wales, incidentally – into south-east Leinster. There was a pre-Patrician shrine founded by Ibar on Begerin in Wexford harbour and it is stated that the Hook area was christianised by followers of the Welsh Brecaun and his family, fellow-workers with St Patrick.[4]

The latter, of course, is believed to have been originally taken to Ireland from south Wales during one of the numerous Irish raids on Roman Britain. This was the period when, for once, the invading was being done by the Irish. The accepted fact that the boy Patrick was taken from the place afterwards known as Milford Haven points to the probability of regular voyaging between Ireland and this particular part of southern Wales.[5]

About AD 800 another people began to appear off the Irish coast – the fierce Norsemen who at first killed and plundered and sailed away again, later settled and built their fortified sea-bases at Dublin, Waterford, Cork, Limerick and Wexford, and finally became merchants and traders. From this era date the settlement of Norsemen (often called Danes) in south Wexford and the founding of Wexford town as a Norse seaport. Outside their walled town they also controlled the area south of Wexford to the coast, which was known as 'the cantred of the Ostmen' and which held the Norsemen's country homes and lands.[6]

These Norse were probably the 'foreign people' to whom Forth was stated to belong in the ninth century.[7] Their presence in the area for a period of three hundred years has left its mark in place-names and in the names of some families. Wexford itself is Norse, meaning 'sandy fjord.' So, too, are the Wexford place-names terminating in 'skar' (a reef of rock, deriving from *sker* or *skjar*) such as Scar, Tuskar and Selskar. Similarly the ending 'ore' (from *öre*, old Scandinavian for 'the sandy point of a promontory') in Carnsore and Cahore, dates from this era. From the Norse emblem of the raven we get Ravensore, Raven's Point, or The Raven (at the entrance to Wexford harbour).

It can be assumed, then, that the inhabitants of south Wexford were a rather mixed lot at the time of the Norman invasion. There were the old Pictish or Celtic tribes with names like O hAirtghoile (Hartly) in Bargy and O Caomhanach (Cavanagh) in Shelmalier; Norse-Celtic tribes like the O Lorcain (Larkins) of Forth, the O Duibhginn (Duggans) of Bargy and Shelburne and the O Laffan (Laffans) of the Hook area, and probably purely Norse pockets in the town of Wexford itself and in places around the coast where the people bore names like Dubhghaill (Doyle), Godfrey, Godkin, Broaders and Cosgrave.

Undoubtedly the Norsemen of Wexford town and cantred were more numerous and variously named than is suggested by the few cognomens chosen here, but of these few we are certain, because their descendants still live in south Wexford today. Thus as one historian has pointed out, 'the Norman invaders found a race of Dano-Irish, deriving from Milesian, ancient British and Scandinavian progenitors'.[8] Apart from the Norse, who were traders and seafarers, the bulk of the scattered tribes existed in the forest clearings by hunting, fishing, primitive farming and cow-herding.

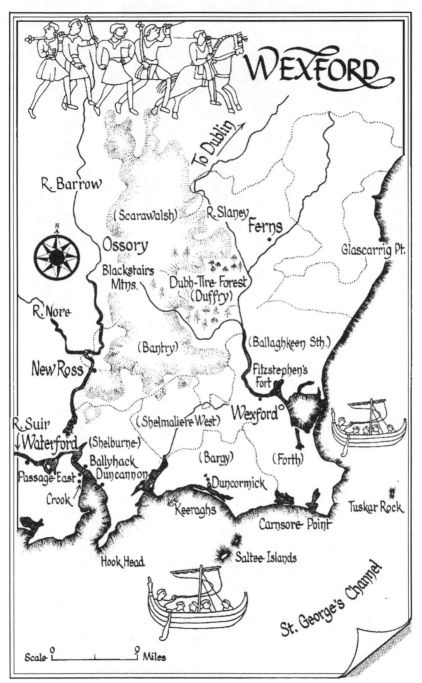

WEXFORD

To Dublin

R. Barrow

(Scarawalsh)   R. Slaney

Ossory   Ferns

Blackstairs   Glascarrig Pt.
Mtns.   Dubh-Tire Forest
             (Duffry)

R. Nore

                (Ballaghkeen Sth.)
(Bantry)
                    Fitzstephen's
New Ross   Fort

R. Suir   (Shelmaliere West)   Wexford°
↓Waterford (Shelburne-)
Passage East   Ballyhack   (Bargy)   (Forth)
            Duncannon
Crook'   •Duncormick
                    Keeraghs   Tuskar Rock
                              Carnsore Point

    Hook Head   Saltee Islands

                                    St. George's Channel

Scale 0 _____ 9 Miles

12 Map of Wexford and south-east

So much for the people who first bore the brunt of the Norman invasion. What of the social and political situation in Ireland as a whole, a situation which of itself, more than any other factor, bred the set of circumstances which led to the invasion? And what of the people who comprised the society which was to be disrupted by the invaders?

Ireland at the time was almost entirely forested, with much of the central plain consisting of bogland and swamp. The people lived in small settlements in cleared areas on the slopes of mountains and hills, on the banks of rivers and along the coast. The only towns were those founded and maintained by the Norse, the Irish themselves living in their rural settlements in houses made of wood protected by circular banks and trenches. The dwellings of kings or chiefs were often built of stone, like the house of Dermot MacMurrough at Ferns. Around these stone houses on their raised mounds were grouped

*13 Cormac's Chapel,
Cashel (left)*

*14 West door, Clonfert
Cathedral (right)*

the timber dwellings of the dependants, forming a village
of sorts. The churches and monasteries of the time were
almost all of stone and surviving ruins, such as King
Cormac's Chapel at Cashel (built 1130), Turlough
O'Connor's church at Tuam and the door of Clonfert
Cathedral, afford good examples of the high standards in
church architecture attained by the medieval Irish.

There were five principal social classes in the country at
the time – the kings of various grades, the nobles, the freemen with property, the freemen with little or no property,
and the non-free classes. The latter classes, which
included slaves and tenants-at-will, formed the majority
of the populace and, together with the serfs, were the
hewers of wood and drawers of water, the people who
provided the food and the essential services of the day for
the upper classes.

Irish society, thus, was frankly aristocratic, with certain
resemblances to the feudalistic system which was to be
brought in by the Normans. Society was based on the

blood-tie or kinship and was organised according to
degrees of blood relationship, its basis being the family.
The basic social grouping was the *fine*, in which all were
related by blood within certain recognised degrees. The
fine was also the basis of succession. The sept was a larger
grouping in which all were descended from common
parents long since dead, all with the same surname, and
all related to some degree by blood.

Several septs or clans together formed a tribe, the
original political unit occupying an area known as a *tuath*.
There were about 185 such *tuatha* in Ireland, most of
which were ruled by so-called kings.[9] Loyalty was thus
based on kinship, the chiefs being heads of powerful
families allied in blood to the king himself. Succession to
such kingships was not, however, hereditary, although it
was essential that a potential king should be of kindred
blood to his subjects. The king or chief was always elected
or chosen from members of the *derb-fine* or 'true family',

15 *Ceremony of conferring kingship*

but the right of succession was limited by law to male descendants, down to great-grandsons, of a reigning king or chief. The system gave rise to countless disputes, ruining many famous families, and compared unfavourably with the Anglo-Norman law of succession in the eldest son.

Claims on the kingship by women or through women were disallowed, a factor which arose later in the case of Strongbow, who assumed the kingship of Leinster through his marriage with Aoife, daughter of Dermot MacMurrough, and thereby incurred the wrath of the rightful claimants to that ill-fated throne.

The people of the time, whose numbers probably did not exceed a quarter of a million, lived by farming and stock-raising, fishing and hunting. The country's mild and moist climate and its plentiful grass made it eminently suitable for breeding cattle, horses, sheep and pigs. Giraldus recorded that 'the tillage land is exuberantly

16 and 17 Irish dress

rich, the fields yielding large crops of corn, herds of cattle graze on the mountains, the woods abound with wild animals'. But he added that, while the crops promised good yields, 'the granaries only show scanty returns'. Giraldus blames the 'excessive rain' for this.

The Irish, however, did not depend chiefly on the wheat, oats, rye and barley which they sowed, for their food. Besides bread they used meat, fish, cheese, butter, fruit, nuts and vegetables, and were fond of milk and mead. Their diet, apparently, was a healthy one because Giraldus (no lauder of the Irish) says that the young

18 May – tending sheep

people grew tall, with handsome figures and fresh complexions. Men's beards, however, were 'barbarous'. The people wore woollen clothes, made by the women from the wool of their own sheep – a sort of cape over a cloak reaching below the knees, with trews and leather-thonged footwear. The clothes were mostly black or grey, he says, the same colour as the sheeps' wool.

In war they wore no armour or defensive gear, and on horseback used no saddle or stirrup. Their roads were few and those few were mere tracks through the mountains and forests. The land was held chiefly by the great families, with portions being acquired from time to time by the professional men like *breithimh* (judges), chroniclers or physicians as fees for their services. Much of the land held by the tribes was commonage on which cattle were grazed, while the arable and meadow lands were divided among the freemen who paid rentals in kind.

Cattle, however, formed the chief wealth of the medieval Irish and were used almost like currency, to pay tributes and fines, rents, dowries and so on. For a pastoral people they had attained considerable artistic and musical standards, for which Giraldus finds faint praise. Some other aspects of the medieval Irish scene did not, however, meet with his approval, notably the lax marriage customs of the time. Husband and wife, for instance, could separate by mutual consent at any time and re-marry. A husband could also repudiate his wife and bring a new one into his home. Concubinage was common. The three marriages of Gormfhlaith, sister of Maelmordha, king of Leinster – to the Danish king of Dublin, Malachy II, high-king of Ireland, and Brian Boru successively – afford an example which must have seemed extremely reprehensible to a Welsh-Norman ecclesiastic.

The custom of fosterage among the chiefs and nobles was also a peculiarly Irish one. Sons of noble families were fostered in other noble families away from home, a practice which in later years, when adopted by some of

19 March – digging and sowing

the Anglo-Norman border barons, led to the sons growing
up as young Irishmen. Fosterage with the Irish then became a crime for the Normans.

Socially and politically, Ireland, 'a wet, wooded island
with which few were concerned and then only for raiding
and despoliation', remained outside the sphere of Con-
tinental influences.[10] While the rest of Europe organised
itself, at times bloodily, under centralised monarchies,
society in Ireland remained largely structured on the
tribal system. The 180 odd tribes were never organised on
a permanent basis. There was constant realignment
among them, actuated by immediate interests, personal
ambitions or jealousies, even by long-standing revenge or
vindictiveness. Intertribal warfare was a chief feature of
Irish life in the era immediately preceding the coming of
the Normans.

The country's isolation from European influences was,
however, a mixed blessing. Though the country had never
been invaded or colonised by the Romans, consequently
never experiencing Roman law and government together

21 September – pasturing swine

20 July – haymaking

with the concomitant Pax Romana (Roman peace), conversely it had never felt the brutal impact of the barbarian hordes which followed the collapse of Roman power elsewhere in Europe.

This breathing space, if such the comparatively peaceful seventh and eighth centuries can be called, afforded the country the opportunity to advance remarkably in culture and learning. This was the golden age of early Christian Ireland when it was truly an island of saints and scholars. This also was one of the two eras in Irish history (the other, strangely enough, being the hundred and fifty years immediately before the Norman invasion) when the strong possibility existed of a Celtic state emerging in Ireland which would be an example to the rest of the world.

As Goddard Orpen put it:

> Had Ireland been allowed to go her way unheeded by Europe, she might in time, and after much suffering, have evolved a better ordered system with some hope of progress in it, and the world might have seen a Celtic

22 December – threshing and winnowing

civilisation where Celtic imagination and Celtic genius, free and unfettered, would assuredly have contributed something towards the solution of human problems, which, as it is, mankind has missed for ever.[11]

But this was not to be. The Norsemen came burning, plundering and killing. The Irish, with their loose tribal system, were not capable of effective resistance. Paradoxically this was the very failing which saved them – there being no national army to destroy, no capital city to subjugate. There was, besides, little for the Norse to plunder except in the scattered monastic centres. Gradually, as they found trading with the Irish more rewarding than plundering them, the Norsemen built their sea-bases at anchorages round the coast, fortified them and settled there, becoming Christians and traders instead of pagans and pirates.

But the effect of the Norse on Irish history was a lasting one. The progress of Celtic civilisation was halted and Celtic literature and culture generally suffered an irreparable loss in the burning and looting of monastic centres with their precious books and treasures. Politically, while the external threat of the Norse had fostered internal unity among the Irish, this was dissipated when the pirates became traders and the Norse role became subordinate in the renewed power struggle between the kings and subkings of Ireland. Finally, when Norse and dissident Irish made a last bid for supremacy at Clontarf in 1014 and when Brian Boru was killed, there died with him the brightest hope for the establishment of a unified Celtic nation. Even under the next external threat, that of the Normans, this hope never returned in full measure.

The next hundred and fifty years, while witnessing an unusual flowering of cultural activity and the arts, saw also a return to tribal dissension and warfare, a return to 'the turmoil of intertribal conflicts (which) has been the despair of writers who seek to tell a connected story.'[12]

23 *The Breac Maedhóig*

Yet try to tell a connected story we shall have to, since an understanding of these intertribal conflicts is essential to our comprehension of the Leinster kings' alliances with the Norsemen, of the enmity between Dermot Mac-Murrough and Tiernan O'Rourke of Breifne, and of Dermot's 'expulsion' and appeal to King Henry II for assistance.

3

Turmoil

The annalists tell us that from the middle of the fifth to the middle of the eleventh century the kings of Leinster (the present-day county of Wexford, with parts of Kildare, Carlow and Wicklow) nearly always belonged to the groups of tribes which congregated round the Curragh of Kildare.[1] But these kings rarely had any effective jurisdiction over the tribes of Uí Ceinnsealaigh who lived in an area which roughly corresponded with the modern diocese of Ferns in south Leinster.[2]

Conversely, when Uí Ceinnsealaigh gave kings to Leinster, they were often opposed by the tribes of north Leinster and Ossory. One consequence of the rivalry was the alliance of the men of north Leinster with the Norse against High-King Brian at Clontarf. But there were other reasons, too, for the enmity between Leinster generally and the high-kings of Ireland. For the chief of these reasons we must go back as far as the first century AD.

At that time Tuathal Teachtmhar carved himself a new kingdom – Meath – by taking slices off several other provinces. Tuathal established the dynasty of Tara which exercised tremendous power over the tribes of the central plain for a long time. He is also said to have originated the controversial *borumha* or cattle tribute which for five hundred years was the cause of countless battles between the kings of Tara and the people of Leinster: 'The traditional cause of the *borumha* was an act of treachery on the part of the king of Laighin (Leinster) towards Tuathal, in revenge for which the latter imposed a heavy tribute

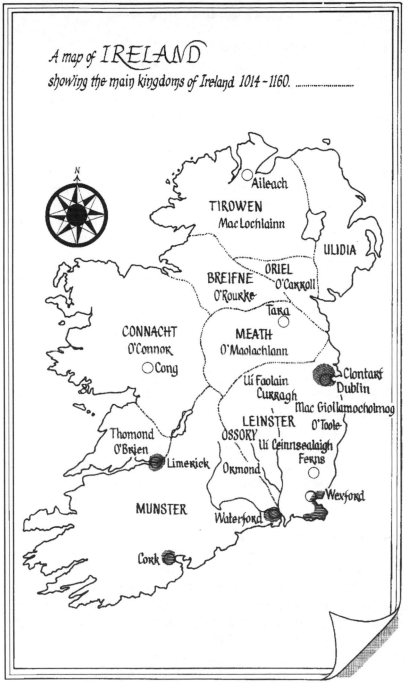

A map of IRELAND

showing the main kingdoms of Ireland 1014 – 1160. ....

N

Aileach

TIROWEN
Mac Lochlainn

ULIDIA

ORIEL
BREIFNE O'Carroll
O'Rourke

Tara

CONNACHT
O'Connor
MEATH
○Cong O'Maolachlann

Clontarf
Uí Faolain Dublin
Curragh
Mac Giollamocholmog
LEINSTER O'Toole
Thomond OSSORY
O'Brien Uí Ceinnsealaigh
●Limerick Ormond Ferns
○

Wexford
MUNSTER
Waterford

Cork●

24 Map of Ireland pre 1169

upon the people of Leinster.'[3]

The possession of Tara itself, or rather the title of king of Tara, appears to have been another bone of contention between Leinster and Meath (Tara may have had religious as well as political significance) and we find the Uí Néill kings of Meath and Connacht and the kings of Leinster in constant dispute over the title, even when Tara itself was a deserted grass-grown site.

The *borumha* was abolished in AD 680 at the behest of St Moling but the bitter memory continued for centuries to influence the relationships between the kings of Leinster and those claiming the title of high-king. I say those 'claiming' the title because for a period of about a hundred and twenty years, from the death in 1022 of Malachy, who had resumed the crown wrested from him by Brian Boru, to 1166 (the year of Dermot MacMurrough's 'expulsion'), there were no nationally recognised high-kings of Ireland, only kings 'with opposition'.

One of the provincial kings, incidentally, who was powerful enough to be reckoned by some as king of Ireland was Dermot MacMael na mBo, king of Leinster and Dublin, who was killed in 1072.[4] He was Dermot Mac-Murrough's ancestor.

This is the period referred to as '. . . one of violence, confusion and turmoil. We read of quarrels between kings and between chieftains, of the mutilation of rivals by blinding or in some other way, of military hostings, of burnings of dwellings and church buildings, of forays and battles, and of violent deaths.'[5]

Throughout all of this we must endeavour to keep track of Dermot MacMurrough and follow his career up to the time he fled to Wales. We must also watch for the crossing of Dermot's path with that of Tiernan O'Rourke, the one-eyed king (or prince) of Breifne (the ancient kingdom which comprised modern County Longford and the southern half of County Leitrim).

Upon the death of Eanna MacMurrough, king of

Leinster, in 1126, Turlough Mor O'Connor, king of Connacht, who had subjugated most of the subkings of Munster and divided their territories among his own nominees, made a foray into Leinster, deposed 'the son of MacMurrough' (presumably Dermot) and set up his own son Conor as king of Leinster and Dublin. Later that year the men of Munster and Leinster rose in joint revolt against Turlough. The Leinstermen deposed his son Conor but later had to accept another O'Connor nominee. Dermot, however, and his south Leinstermen were not prepared to bow to an O'Connor overlord, so that Turlough, aided by Tiernan O'Rourke, had to make a foray into Uí Ceinnsealaigh in 1128. He marched to Wexford, thence round Leinster to Dublin.

The annals say he wrought great destruction of cows and add a most significant sentence from our point of view: 'The ill fame of that hosting rested on Tiernan O'Rourke.'[6] The paths of Dermot and Tiernan had crossed; the wheels of fate had been set in motion.

Despite a defeat at the hands of the men of Ossory in 1134, Dermot grew in power and importance. Later in 1134, aided by the Norse of Dublin (the old alliance again)

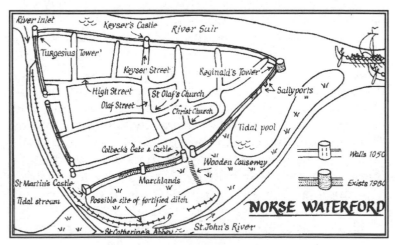

25 Norse Waterford, c. 1050

he avenged himself on the Ossory men who were assisted by the Norse of Waterford. Three years later, once more aided by the Norse of Dublin and Wexford with a fleet of 200 ships, he laid siege to Waterford and exacted hostages. About the same time he made a treaty with Murrough O Maolachlann (O Melaghlin), king of Meath, whereby Dermot undertook to go to Murrough's aid 'against any one with as great an army', provided that Murrough would be pleased to suffer him (Dermot) to enjoy without disturbance the territories of the Uí Faolain and Offaly.

In 1138, in pursuance of this treaty, Dermot went to the aid of Murrough against the powerful alliance of Turlough O'Connor, Tiernan O'Rourke and Donough O'Carroll of Oriel. The two armies camped for a week confronting each other but eventually dispersed without a battle.

It is a measure of Dermot's power at the time that O'Connor and O'Rourke hesitated to engage him in battle. Dermot now was certainly someone to be reckoned with in the southern part of Ireland. He was, as king of Uí Ceinnsealaigh, the largest kingdom of Leinster, rated chief king of that province. In fact, a memorandum in the *Book of Leinster* describes him as the high-king of Leath-Mhogha (the southern half of the country). He may even have had his eye on the high-kingship of Ireland.

But he had enemies within his own borders. Among them were Donal MacFaolain, Murtough MacGiollamocholmog and Murchadh O'Toole, chiefs of the traditionally rival north Leinster tribes, who undoubtedly resented Dermot's overlordship. Treacherously and cold-bloodedly Dermot got rid of them – by killing or blinding. The annals tell us that in the year 1141 seventeen of the kingfolk of Leinster, including the three mentioned above, were 'removed' for him in this way by his brother Murrough, an act which, in the words of one chronicler, 'brought all Leinster far under hand'.

'Thus,' says Orpen, 'did Dermot, like many of his

compeers, secure his throne with the corpses and pierced eye-balls of his rivals.'[7]

Dermot's growing power was being viewed with anything but favour by other provincial kings. In 1141 a great army led by the O'Briens of Thomond raided first Connacht and then Leinster as far as Wexford town.[8] Again, in the following year, while Dermot was engaged in a march with Turlough O'Connor (in which he was probably a most unwilling participator) his own territory of Uí Ceinnsealaigh was once more raided by an O'Brien.

Meanwhile, Turlough O'Connor was advancing towards his objective – the high-kingship. He was, undoubtedly, the most powerful man in Ireland at this time. He is one of the kings for whom the supremacy was claimed[9] and it was said that he was one of the most outstanding of all the kings since Brian Boru.[10]

We find him at this time taking Murrough O Maolachlann, king of Meath, prisoner and giving his kingdom first to his own son Conor O'Connor (who was killed within the year by one of his new subjects) and then dividing it between Tiernan O'Rourke and Dermot MacMurrough. This explosive arrangement, as might be expected, lasted only a year.

The uneasy situation coincided with a church-inspired peace throughout Ireland, agreed to in 1144, but this also lasted only a year, so that in 1145 we find the annalists recording 'great war, so that Ireland was a trembling sod'.

Now a new contender for the high-kingship appeared on the scene – Muircertach MacLochlainn, king of Aileach in the north and representative of the ancient claims of the northern Uí Néill to the overlordship of Ireland. After several campaigns between the years 1147 and 1149 he subdued Ulidia (Ulster), Oriel and other parts in Leath Chonn (the northern half of the century). Next Tiernan O'Rourke and then Dermot MacMurrough submitted to him and by 1150 he was being styled king of Ireland.[11] In that year he made a royal journey into Meath where the

26 The grianan of Aileach

hostages of Connacht were brought to him – signifying the submission of that province – and he divided Meath between Turlough O'Connor, Tiernan O'Rourke and O'Carroll.

Two years later Turlough and MacLochlainn, who had been eyeing each other suspiciously, decided to call a truce. Once more they divided Meath, this time sharing it with Dermot MacMurrough. Then there occurred the next fateful event in the chain of happenings that led to the Norman invasion. Tiernan O'Rourke refused to accept the new division of Meath and he was crushed by the all-powerful alliance of MacLochlainn, O'Connor and Mac-Murrough. His own territory of Breifne was taken from him. Taken also on this occasion was his wife Dervorgilla. The abductor was Dermot MacMurrough. The wheels of fate now began to whirl rapidly.

4
Abduction

To the antipathy and rivalry which existed between Dermot MacMurrough and Tiernan O'Rourke there was now added, in no small measure, a personal hatred that overwhelmed all other feelings. Dermot had revenged himself on O'Rourke for the latter's depredations in Uí Ceinnsealaigh in 1128, but in such a manner that the Breifne king was shamed before the men of Ireland. This insult was far worse than the injury suffered through the loss of his territory and its searing fire continued to burn within him for long afterwards.

In many ways he and MacMurrough were alike; they were both violent, unscrupulous men, easily swayed by impulse, passion and ambition. It may not be out of place to disrupt our narrative here and sketch the careers and characters of these two.

MacMurrough, son of Donncadh MacMurrough, king of Uí Ceinnsealaigh, was born in 1110. He was only five when his father was killed in a battle at Dublin by Donal, son of Murtough O'Brien of Thomond, and the Norse of Dublin.[1]

Giraldus, however, relates that the citizens of Dublin murdered Dermot's father while he was sitting in the hall of one of his chief men which he used for his court of justice, and the citizens, as a measure of their distaste, buried a dead dog with his body.

Donncadh was succeeded by another member of his family and then by his son Eanna who died in 1126. Eanna was succeeded by Dermot as king of Uí Ceinnsealaigh. He was then just over sixteen years of age.[2]

Born into a warring environment he could hardly have escaped the effects of an upbringing in which killing, savagery and hatred were commonplace. He is usually described as cruel and turbulent, even in an age notorious for its cruelty and turbulence.

Giraldus, who was acquainted with many who knew Dermot, particularly in his closing years, has left this description of him:

> Dermot was tall of stature and of stout build. A man of warlike spirit and a brave one in his nation, with a voice hoarse from frequent shouting in the din of battle. One who preferred to be feared rather than to be loved, who was obnoxious to his own people and an object of hatred to strangers. His hand was against every man, and every man's hand against his.[3]

A footnote in the Bryan Geraghty edition of the *Annals of the Four Masters* (1846) adds a little more to the picture:

> His character is drawn by various writers in the darkest colours; he was rapacious, fierce, cruel, vindictive, and of violent passions; though to gain popularity he endeavoured to conciliate the lower classes of people. It appears he was a man of great stature and strength of body, and possessed of much personal bravery.

One example of the ugly extremes to which Dermot could go to gain his ends is given by the annalists.[4] When Donal MacFaolain was set up as king by Turlough O'Connor, fighting took place between the tribes of Offaly and Uí Faolain as to which of the two tribes should have the appointment of the new abbess of Kildare, and Cearbhall, the new king's brother, was killed. Three years later, Dermot appears to have settled the question 'in a peculiarly revolting fashion'.[5] He and the men of Uí Ceinnsealaigh took and burned the house of the abbess 'and the

27 *Dermot MacMurrough*

nun herself was carried off a prisoner and put into a man's bed'. The motive for this dastardly deed was, apparently, to incapacitate her from holding office.

Yet, for all that, Dermot was capable of arousing great loyalty among his own family and followers. He was married to Mor, only daughter of Murtough O'Toole, king of Uí Muireadhaigh (whose territory embraced the southern half of the modern County Kildare). Mor's brother was Lorcan O'Toole, abbot of Glendalough, who later became archbishop of Dublin. Lorcan, therefore, was Dermot's brother-in-law.

Dermot apparently had six children – Donal Cavanagh (an illegitimate son who was fostered by the Cavanaghs of Kilcavan, near Ferns), Eanna (ancestor of the Kinsellas of Uí Ceinnsealaigh), Conor (who was blinded by an enemy in 1168 and put to death by High-King Ruairi O'Connor in 1170), and daughters Aoife (who married Strongbow), Urlacam (who married Donal O'Brien, king of Thomond, and Dervorgil (who married Donal Mac-Giollamocholmog, a minor king whose territory lay south-west of Dublin).[6]

For a man reputedly so savage and irreligious Dermot was a munificent patron of the Church and of the arts. He founded the Cistercian abbey at Baltinglass, the convent of St Mary de Hogges near Dublin, and the priory of All Hallows (where Trinity College, Dublin, now stands). He endowed the priory with the lands of Baldoyle and in 1161 he founded and endowed the Augustinian monastery at Ferns, the beautiful ruins of which still stand. It was in this monastery, incidentally, that he took refuge in 1166 after his defeat by Ruairi O'Connor, having burnt his house to prevent it falling into other hands.

As a patron of the arts Dermot was responsible for the compilation of the *Book of Leinster*, which was the chief treasure of his library. He also employed as his Latin writer Morice Regan, who seemingly lived to tell the remarkable tale retold by the author of *The Song of Dermot*.

Dermot's chief claim to notoriety, however, rests on his invitation to the foreigners to invade Ireland. For this act his name has passed into history as being synonymous with treachery. For this he has become known as *Diarmuid na nGall*, Dermot of the Foreigners.

Tiernan O'Rourke matched MacMurrough in violence and lack of scruples. Although his wife Dervorgilla was a daughter of Murrough O Maolachlann, king of Meath, O'Rourke was constantly embroiled in fighting against the O Maolachlanns, though the alliance between Murrough and Dermot MacMurrough may have been a factor here.

28 *Deed confirming grant of land*

Like MacMurrough, O'Rourke and his family suffered in the tribal wars. A son of his was killed in battle in 1124, while he himself was expelled by his own subjects in 1140 (he regained the chieftainship later). At the time of the 'abduction' of his wife in 1152 he must have been at least sixty years of age.

Dervorgilla herself was forty-four, while Dermot was forty-two at the time. But let our contemporary chroniclers and the annalists tell the story.

The author of *The Song of Dermot* wrote:

> But O'Rourke, the rich king
> Had a beautiful wife at the time
> The daughter of King Melaghlinn . . .
> Dermot, king of Leinster
> Whom this lady loved so much
> Made pretence to her of loving
> While he did not love her at all
> But only wished to the utmost of his power
> To avenge, if he could, the great shame
> Which the men of Leath-Cuinn wrought of old
> On the men of Leath-Mhogha in his territory:
> King Dermot often sent word
> To the lady whom he so loved
> By letter and by messenger
> Often did the king send word
> That she was altogether, in truth,
> The thing in the world that he most loved.

The poet's statement that Dermot 'often sent word' to Dervorgilla suggests a correspondence of some duration. This is borne out by the Irish historian Geoffrey Keating who, writing about 1630, said: 'There had indeed been an illicit attachment between them for many years previously.'[7]

The Abbé MacGeoghegan, in his *History of Ireland* published in Paris in 1758, says that Dervorgilla, in fact, had married O'Rourke against her will: 'This princess

29 Baltinglass Abbey

indulged a secret passion for Dermot, king of Leinster,
who paid his addresses to her before her marriage.' If this
be the case Dervorgilla was merely returning to her first
love when she eloped with Dermot – for an elopement it
was, not an abduction.

   The Song of Dermot continues:

>   *And the lady sent him word*
>   *By a secret messenger*
>   *That she would do all his will:*
>   *To the king who is so renowned*
>   *She returns answer again.*
>   *Both by word of mouth and by letter*
>   *That he should come for her in such manner*
>   *With all the host of Leinster*
>   *And by force and by war*
>   *Should carry her away with him from the land.*

Dervorgilla, as is clearly indicated, was by no means an
unwilling victim. In fact, we are told that one of the
messages she sent to Dermot contained the information

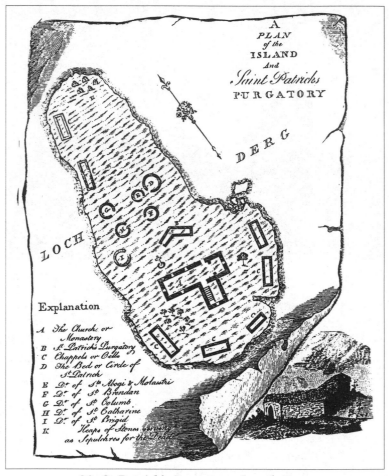

30 *St Patrick's Purgatory, Lough Derg*

that her husband Tiernan had gone on a pilgrimage to the
cave of Patrick's Purgatory (on Lough Derg, County Donegal) and that therefore he 'would have an opportunity of
quietly carrying her with him to Leinster'.[8]

Whether this was the case or not we cannot be sure. The
annalists say that the 'abduction' took place on the occasion of O'Rourke's defeat by the powerful triumvirate of
MacLochlainn, Turlough O'Connor and MacMurrough,

but it may have taken place shortly after that when O'Rourke, bereft of his territory, went on a pilgrimage of penance to Lough Derg. It is even possible that Dervorgilla was not above a little subterfuge to ensure her 'abduction' by Dermot, and what better way to entice a lover than to say, in effect, 'Husband away, come today.'

She was, at any rate, prepared for the event. *The Song of Dermot* says that Dermot assembled his men and reached the place of assignation (said to be Drumahaire, County Leitrim, where O'Rourke had his stronghold):

> *Where the lady had sent word*
> *That she would be ready.*

Dervorgilla played her part well. 'The woman wept and screamed in pretence, as if Diarmuid were carrying her off by force,' writes Keating.[9] Yet she had, apparently, arranged that she would not be abducted empty-handed. The annals state that her cattle and furniture went with her, 'the lady consenting to the abduction and her own brother Maolachlann, the new king of Meath, instigating Dermot to the act for some abuses of her husband, Tiernan, done to her before'.[10]

We do not know what these abuses were. We do know that Tiernan himself now felt abused. 'O'Rourke bitterly complained,' says *The Song of Dermot*, but how many listened with compassion?

Goddard Orpen, perhaps, supplies an answer:

> It is impossible that in an age of lawless violence, treachery and loose sexual relations, this elopement or abduction of a faithless wife could have been regarded as a very serious moral offence. To O'Rourke, however, it was a grievous personal insult, and one which he seems never to have forgotten or forgiven. That it was the sole cause of Dermot's expulsion fourteen years afterwards, as stated both by Giraldus and by the writer of *The Song of Dermot*, and affirmed by some of the Irish

annals, is, considering the lapse of time, too much to assert; but by making a mortal enemy of Tiernan O'Rourke, who, as we shall see, was the actual agent of Dermot's expulsion, it directly contributed to that result, and we cannot wonder that the popular imagination should have exaggerated the personal element in the cause, and that a later age should have seen a dramatic fitness in the consequence.[11]

Apropos Orpen's reference to the loose sexual relations of the time he adds a footnote: 'In this same year (1152) the great Synod of Kells, under Cardinal Paparo, found it necessary to pass enactments against concubinage and irregular unions.'

The idyll of Dermot and Dervorgilla at Ferns was short-lived.[12] In the following year, 1163, Tiernan O'Rourke having made his peace with Turlough O'Connor, the latter marched against Dermot, took away Dervorgilla (and her cattle) and restored her to her husband. The annals say she returned to Tiernan and there seems no reason to doubt that she continued to live with him.[13]

In later life Dervorgilla seemingly sought to make atonement for the errors of her ways because she became a noted benefactress of the Church. She endowed, in 1157, the newly consecrated church of the Cistercian abbey at Mellifont, near Drogheda, giving 'three score ounces of gold, and a chalice of gold on the altar of Mary, and a cloth for each of the nine other altars that were in that church'.[14] Her husband Tiernan was among the distinguished attendance on that occasion.

She is mentioned again, in 1167, as being responsible for building the Church of the Nuns at Clonmacnoise – a beautiful structure which speaks well for her taste in architecture. In 1186 she retired to the monastery at Mellifont where she died in 1193 at the age of eighty-five.

As we have seen she was forty-four at the time of her abduction – old enough, one might assume, to have

31 *The Nuns' Church, Clonmacnoise*

known better. The fact that neither she nor Dermot was in the first flush of youthful passion at the time makes one believe that their 'illicit attachment' may have been a long-standing one and that its climax, the 'abduction', may have had political undertones involving her own brother.

Arthur Ua Clerigh puts forward another theory which is worth quoting: 'The effect of all the entries (in the *Annals*) is, in our judgment, that Derbhforgaill was taken away for safety, and as a hostage, with the consent of her family, and that she was restored to Tighernan when he made his submission to Turlough.'[15]

At this remove we can only guess at the motives of the chief actors in the drama. *Autre temps, autre moeurs.* For us Dervorgilla and indeed Dermot and Tiernan, for all we know about them, must remain shadowy, enigmatic figures playing out their roles in the most dramatic scenes in Irish history.

32 Mellifont Abbey

5

Exile

Fourteen years were to elapse between the Dervorgilla episode and Dermot's flight into exile. In that period the Leinster king's fortunes rose and sank in the turmoil of the intertribal struggles for supremacy, before plunging finally to their nadir in 1166.

In 1153 we find Dermot releasing from captivity Niall O'Moore, chief of Laoighis, after he had been blinded to prevent him from assuming power again. Here again we witness Dermot's apparent cruelty and unscrupulousness but we should remember that the blinding of enemies or rivals was a common practice in Ireland then.[1]

To blind a chief – or, worse, to castrate him, rendering him incapable of having issue – was a barbaric method of ensuring that he was incapable of ruling. It was perpetrated by many kings and chieftains of the time. Maolachlann O Maolachlann, who claimed to be sole king of Meath on the death of his father Murrough, blinded his nephew to put an end to his claim on the kingship; Tadhg O'Brien, who had been installed as king of half Munster by Turlough O'Connor, was blinded by his brother to prevent him from reigning; even Turlough O'Connor himself blinded his own son Hugh in 1136, probably because he considered him a threat to his throne; and Ruairi O'Connor, Turlough's son, on succeeding to the kingship, blinded his brother to prevent him claiming the title. Thus Dermot was being no crueller than many of his fellow-kings in twelfth-century Ireland. Nor, indeed, were the unsettled conditions in the country much different from those in Britain and France when these countries were in the birth-throes of nationhood and some time before. Internal upheaval and intertribal warfare, with the consequent survival of the strongest, were commonplace at the time.

The principal contestants for the overlordship of the country now were the O'Connors of Connacht and the MacLochlainns of Aileach in the north. When Turlough O'Connor died in 1156, being succeeded by his son Ruairi, there was a reshuffle of alliances. Muircertach MacLochlainn and Ruairi cast around for new allies and got them, by persuasion or force.

Ruairi established an alliance with Tiernan O'Rourke. MacLochlainn took hostages from Dermot MacMurrough and, in return, gave Dermot the entire province of Leinster as his own. Once again O'Rourke and MacMurrough were to be found on opposite sides.

The inevitable confrontation between MacLochlainn and O'Connor took place in 1159 when, in a great battle at Ardee, the northmen routed Ruairi with 'dreadful slaughter'. MacLochlainn asserted his supremacy over nearly all of Ireland but O'Connor was not yet crushed. If he could not beat MacLochlainn on the field of battle perhaps he could win at the peace table; in pursuit of this aim he met MacLochlainn at Assaroe with a view to calling a truce. But they failed to reach an agreement.

The manoeuvring restarted. In 1161 O'Connor and O'Rourke invaded Meath but were checked by Mac-Lochlainn to whom they were forced to give hostages.

Dermot, at this time, exercised undisputed sway over all Leinster and was held in high regard (in spite of recent misdemeanours) by both laity and clergy. In 1162, under his patronage and protection, a synod of the Irish Church was held at Clane, County Kildare, when, among other things, 'the scandalous custom' whereby the see of Patrick at Armagh passed by hereditary succession for fifteen generations, and in eight cases had been filled by married laymen, was formally abolished.

In that year also, Dermot's brother-in-law, Lorcan O'Toole, was consecrated bishop of Dublin and archbishop of Leinster. Orpen is of the opinion that Lorcan may have owed his elevation to Dermot's influence both with the Norsemen of Dublin and with the northern powers, MacLochlainn and Archbishop Gelasius of Armagh.[2]

A few years later an event of crucial importance occurred: Muircertach MacLochlainn was slain in battle in 1166 and the way was open for the Connacht contender. Ruairi O'Connor, accompanied by O'Rourke and O Maolachlann, marched to Dublin, and was there inaugurated high-king of Ireland – the last, had he but known it: 'This change of dynasty was disastrous for Dermot Mac-Murrough, king of Leinster; for the O'Connor supremacy required a friendly ruler in Leinster such as Mac-Murrough could never be; and furthermore, O'Rourke, who had become an indispensable support of O'Connor power, was bitterly hostile to MacMurrough.'[3]

As soon as O'Connor became high-king he set out, accompanied by the Dublin Norsemen and O'Rourke, to receive the submission of Oriel. Only one man now stood in his way – MacMurrough. So Ruairi marched southwards into Leinster.

There is considerable confusion in the ancient chronicles about the sequence of the next events. Some of the annals say that Dermot, deserted one by one by his subchiefs, tried to make a last stand in the woods of the hilly border area between what are now the counties of Carlow and Wexford. But O'Connor and O'Rourke broke through to Ferns, Dermot's capital, to find it already burning.[4] (Dermot, it appears, set it on fire so that there would be less for his enemies to plunder.) Our annalists continue by stating that Dermot submitted to the high-king and gave him four hostages. He was deposed as king of Leinster but allowed to retain his own hereditary principality of Uí Ceinnsealaigh.

Another annalist says Dermot, even after this defeat and submission, remained defiant in Uí Ceinnsealaigh – but not for long.[5] O'Rourke, bent on revenge, prepared to deliver the *coup de grace*. Aided again by the Norsemen of Dublin and by a new ally, Dermot O Maolachlann of Meath, O'Rourke marched against Dermot. This time there were no half measures, no negotiations. Deserted by almost everyone, Dermot fled. It is most likely that Ruairi O'Connor ordered the second expedition against Dermot, for the *Book of Leinster* says he was banished, not by O'Rourke, but by 'the men of Erin', that is by O'Connor's army.

Dermot's territory of Uí Ceinnsealaigh was divided between Donough MacGiolla Phadraig, king of Ossory, and Dermot's own brother Murchadh, who was set up by O'Connor as king instead of Dermot.[6] The latter's son Conor was taken captive by MacGiolla Phadraig and, in 1168, following Dermot's return with the Normans, was blinded by his captor and put to death two years later by O'Connor.

33 The Dermot entry in the 'Book of Leinster'

An entry in the *Book of Leinster*, probably made by, or done at the dictation of, Aodh MacCrimhthainn,[7] Dermot's tutor, reflects the consternation undoubtedly caused among MacMurrough's followers by the train of events: 'Mary, great is the deed which was done in Ireland today, that is, Diarmait, son of Donnchadh Mac Murchadha,

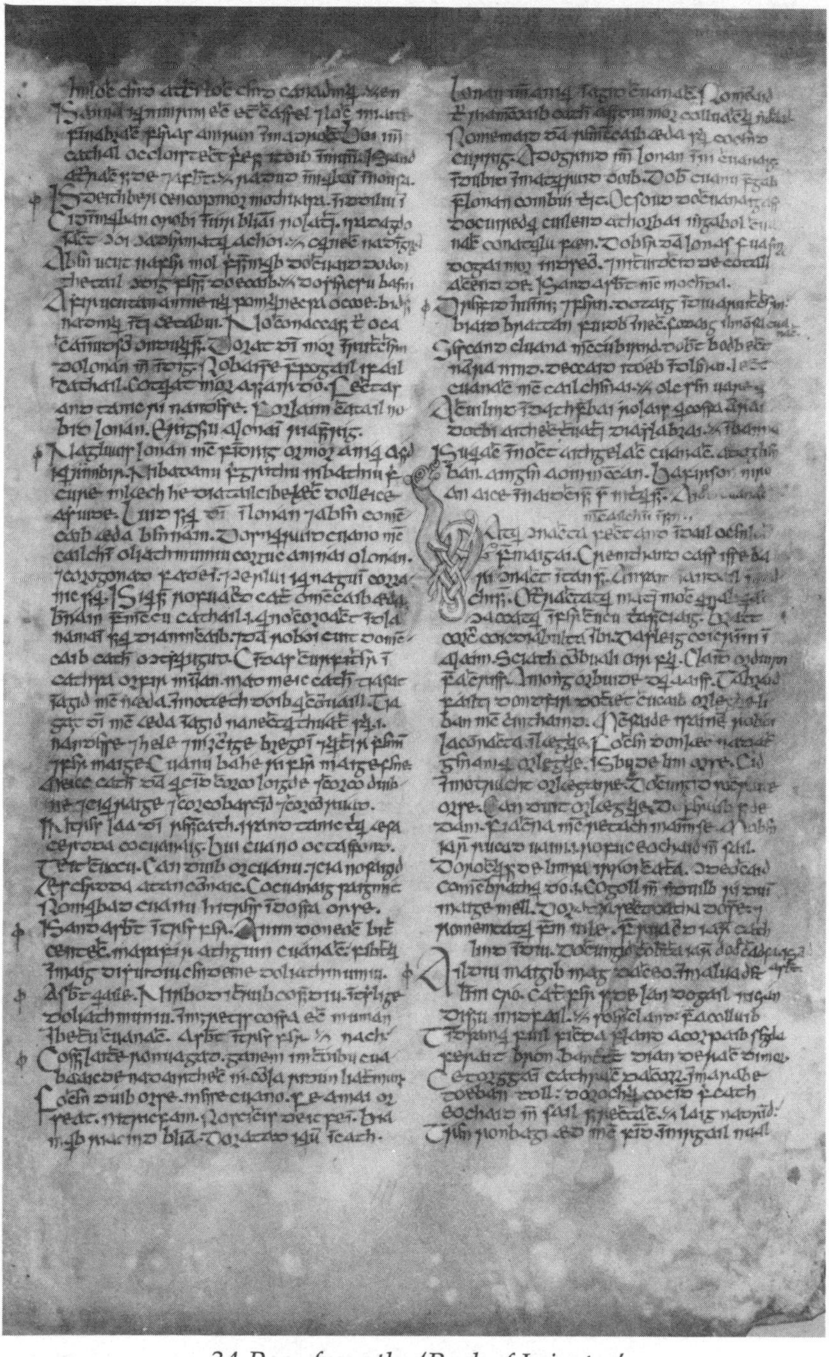

34 Page from the 'Book of Leinster'

king of Leinster and the foreigners was expelled across the sea by the men of Ireland. Alas, alas, O Lord, what will I do?'

Dermot apparently did not leave Ireland immediately. *The Song of Dermot* describes his abandonment by his erstwhile allies, including Murrough O'Brien, 'an evil rebel', whom Dermot tried to meet and rally by various stratagems, including disguising himself as a monk. But all these efforts failed. On 1 August 1166 'he took ship at Corkeran'.[8]

Dermot brought with him 'Auliffe O'Kinad ... and more than sixty-three'. This Auliffe O'Kinad was probably Amhlaeibh Ua Ceinneidigh, lord of Ormond, who had been blinded by Turlough O'Brien, Dermot's enemy, in 1164. Perhaps Amhlaeibh was among the few who remained loyal to Dermot; perhaps Dermot took him along as a form of 'insurance' against the day of his return; perhaps a latent spark of compassion for the blind man flamed within him in his own hour of need.

MacMurrough was the last of the provincial kings who had stood in the way of High-King Ruairi, who now was undisputed overlord of the entire country: 'He celebrated the Tailteann games, and the political structure of Ireland seemed to be restored. But the banished king of Leinster had already found in Wales allies who were to reverse it for ever.[9]

When Dermot sailed for Bristol to seek those allies, he left behind his illegitimate son Donal Cavanagh to protect his few remaining interests. Among those who sailed with him was his beautiful daughter Aoife. She was to play a significant role in the next part of the saga.

6
The Normans

Had Dermot never been expelled, or had he never invoked Norman aid, we must rest assured that the ultimate result would not have been very different – thus Orpen on the probability of the annexation of Ireland by the Normans.[1]

Other historians agree with this view. Curtis says: 'Ireland had already for a century been threatened by the powerful monarchy of Norman England, and still more immediately by the aggressive Norman baronial race. The fall of Celtic Wales heralded the fall of Celtic Ireland.'[2]

Who, then, were these Normans who had conquered England, colonised Wales and now threatened Ireland? They were the descendants of Norsemen who had settled on the banks of the Seine in northern France in the tenth century. The territory which they occupied became known as Normandy and they, in time, as Normans. In 1066, their leader, the then duke of Normandy, better known as William the Conqueror, laid claim to the throne of England, invaded that country and, in a single battle at Hastings, defeated the native English and took over the land.

The French-speaking Norman barons divided the rich pastures among themselves, building great stone castles to protect their holdings. These fortifications were usually manned by Flemish mercenaries, and beneath the grey walls and the menacing bows of the soldiers the native English became mere slaves, terrorised into abject submission by the turbulent barons.

35 Cilgerran Castle

The Normans were not as successful in subduing the Welsh, however. The Cymri, who had maintained their independence against Roman and Saxon, for long withstood the onslaught of the new invaders. In this they were aided by their Celtic brothers in Ireland: again and again Norse and Irish of the east coast had assisted the Welsh, both against the Normans and in their own internal feuds.[3]

But by 1100 most of Wales had been brought under the Norman yoke. In 1109 we find King Henry I (the fourth son of William the Conqueror) granting to Gilbert de Clare 'all the land of Cardigan, if he could win it from the Welsh'. What they could not subdue by the sword the Normans acquired through intermarriage with the Welsh. One Walter FitzOtho, for instance, married Gladys, daughter of the prince of north Wales, and his son Gerald married the famous Nesta, daughter of Rhys ap Tewdwr, prince of Deheubarth (most of south Wales). We are to find the same pattern of military conquest and inter-marriage in the invasion of Ireland.

When not battling the Welsh these Normans and Flemings were often fighting among themselves. Henry had sought to rid himself of them by sending them out to conquer the Welsh 'marches' but they continued to be a threat to his security. It was probably with the idea of des-patching these warring barons and knights to another land that he drew up plans in 1155 for the invasion of Ireland.

He was not the first Norman monarch to contemplate the conquest of Ireland. William the Conqueror himself is said to have pondered on that possibility much earlier but had to defer his plans while he subjugated England. Henry II (grandson of Henry I and great-grandson of the Conqueror) was to be afforded both the opportunity and the men to carry it through. He was a man of tremendous energy and ability, a man who, though king of England, regarded himself more as a Frenchman and spent most of his time in France. He spoke no English, only French, and

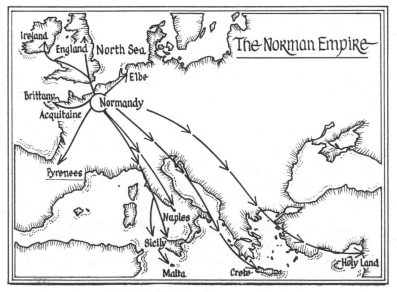

36 *The Norman empire*

his possessions included more than half of the area occupied by France, as well as England, Scotland and Wales.

He was continually moving from one part of his territory to another with a restlessness which has been commented on by many. A French contemporary said of him: 'The king neither walks nor rides; he flies,' and Giraldus has left us this vivid pen-picture of him:

> He had a reddish complexion, rather dark, and a large round head. His eyes were grey, bloodshot, and flashed in anger. He had a fiery countenance, his voice was tremulous, and his neck a little bent forward; but his chest was broad, and his arms were muscular. His body was fleshy, and he had an enormous paunch, rather by the fault of nature than from gross feeding ... In order to reduce and cure, as far as possible, this natural tendency and defect, he waged a continual war, so to speak, with his own belly by taking immoderate exercise ... He took little rest ... he had frequent swellings in his legs and feet, increased much by his violent exercise on horseback, which added to his other complaints ... He was well-learned ... inordinately fond of hawking and hunting.[4]

Giraldus adds a personal comment after remarking that Henry 'could scarcely spare an hour to hear Mass'. 'Would to God,' said the Welshman, 'he had been as zealous in his devotions as he was in his sports.'

Henry, in many ways, typified the Normans whom he ruled. They, too, were restless and turbulent, revelling in the high adventure of war and conquest. Curtis summarises their character thus:

> The dominant genius of the 'Franks' was feudal, military, and romantic. They belonged to the older feudalism, which found its best expression on the borders, but which in England was bridled by the

masterful genius of Henry II. In Wales they could conquer as widely as their swords, carry on private war, invade the Welsh mountaineers and divide the spoil among the barons. This was to be their spirit in Ireland. But it was something the Gaels could understand, and such men before long were to become almost as Irish as the Irish. The feudal class lived also in the tradition of the minstrels and the great *chansons de geste* of Charlemagne, Arthur, and Godfrey; it was no great step for them to delight in the music, language, and ancient epics of Ireland. Nationalism was scarcely known to these men who had come over a century ago as Frenchmen and had not yet become English. Adaptability was their genius, and proud as they were of their own blood, speech and traditions, they were ready to treat as equals any race that they could respect and freely to intermarry with it. In Wales they had absorbed Welsh blood and doubtless knew something of the Celtic speech. In Ireland the first generation of them was only too ready to make 'happy marriages' with Irish princesses.[5]

As well as being skilled in the art of war the Normans

37 *Seal of William I*   38 *Seal of Henry I*

were good administrators, builders and farmers. According to Brian Fitzgerald:

> In the province of Normandy they founded a mighty state, which gradually extended its influence over the neighbouring provinces of Brittany and Maine. And, without laying aside that dauntless valour which terrorised every land from the Elbe to the Pyrenees, the Normans rapidly acquired all, and more than all, the knowledge and refinement which they found in the country where they settled. They established internal order. They adopted the French tongue, in which Latin was the main element, and raised it to a dignity and importance which it has never lost. French literature became the glory of the civilised world. They embraced Christianity and adopted the feudal doctrines of France which they worked into some sort of a system ... They adopted their own form of architecture, the romanesque. They were chivalrous, these Normans; indeed, with them began the age of chivalry ... They were dignified in their bearing and well-spoken. They were born orators as well as born lawyers, just as they were born soldiers. For before all else they were soldiers. Their conquests extended to Southern Italy and Sicily on the one hand, and to the British Isles on the other.[6]

Prominent among the Norman settlers in Wales was a family whose name was to become synonymous with the conquest and with the spread of Norman power in Ireland. The name of this family was FitzGerald. The first bearer of the name was Maurice, founder of the Irish dynasty of the Geraldines, who were to play such an extraordinary part in the subsequent history of Ireland.

The Geraldines were descended from the noble family of the Gherardini of Florence, some of whom had passed by way of France into England and Wales. In England the name became altered to Geraldini and the French prefix *fils* became, under English influence perhaps, the now

39 *Maurice FitzGerald*

familiar Fitz.

Another element among the settlers were the Flemings, descendants of the mercenaries from Flanders planted in south Wales by William the Conqueror. This plantation had been enlarged in 1107 by Henry I. By 1167 many of these Flemings had risen in the feudal ranks and bore knights' escutcheons. For the most part, however, it was Flemish men-at-arms, and Welsh archers, who were to provide the 'shock troops' of the first landings in Ireland, and tough soldiers they were.

Such, then, were the men whose aid Dermot Mac-Murrough sought when he sailed for Bristol in 1166.[7]

40 *Welsh archer*

7

Laudabiliter

Camden describes, in quaint fashion, consideration of an earlier plan to invade Ireland:

> After these tempestuous foraine warres were allaied there followed a most grevious storme of civill dissention at home, which made way for the English to conquer Ireland. For, Henrie the Second, King of England, taking occasion and opportunity, by the privie dislikes, heart-burnings, and malicious emulations among the Irish Princes, grew into a serious deliberation with the Nobles of England in the year of Salvation 1155 about the conquest of Ireland, for the behoofe of his brother William of Anjou: But through the counsel of his mother Mawde the Empresse, this project was rejected unto another time.[1]

The plans were laid before a Council of State at Winchester in 1155 but, because they did not commend themselves to the Empress Matilda, Henry II's mother, the invasion was postponed. The plans were well laid, Henry having sought and been granted a papal privilege to carry out the conquest. This privilege was the so-called bull *Laudabiliter*, which has been the subject of fierce controversy ever since.

The story of *Laudabiliter* is an involved one but it is essential to our narrative to devote some attention to it. Henry had a precedent in seeking the blessing of the pope for his invasion – William the Conqueror had obtained the blessing of Pope Alexander II when he invaded England a

41 *Seal of Empress Matilda*   42 *Seal of Henry II*

century earlier. And with an Englishman on the papal throne what better time to seek a commission to enter Ireland and carry out religious reform!

The Englishman who was pope at the time (and the only Englishman to sit on the papal throne) was Nicholas Breakspeare, who ruled under the title Adrian IV. Son of a poor clerk, he had been a monk of St Alban's and was elected pope in 1154. He died in 1159.

As well as being English, Adrian was also a personal friend of Henry, whom he regarded as the man who had saved England from anarchy. But let Adrian's contemporary, and close friend, the famed scholar John of Salisbury, afterwards bishop of Chartres, tell the story:

> It was at my request that he (Adrian IV) granted to the illustrious King of the English, Henry II, the hereditary possession of Ireland, as his still extant letters attest; for all islands are reputed to belong by a long-established right to the Church of Rome, to which they were granted by Constantine, who established and endowed it. He sent moreover by me to the King a golden ring, adorned by a fine emerald, in token of his investiture with the government of Ireland.[2]

Hanmer's *Chronicle of Ireland* offers confirmation that Henry sent a monk named John of Salisbury and others as a deputation to Rome to solicit this bull from Adrian.[3]

'The long-established right of the Church of Rome to all islands', mentioned by John of Salisbury, refers to the so-called 'Donation of Constantine', which is based on a document of dubious origin.

> By this name is understood, since the end of the Middle Ages, a forged document of Emperor Constantine the Great, by which large privileges and rich possessions were conferred on the Pope and the Roman Church. In the oldest known (ninth century) manuscript (Bibliotheque Nationale, Paris, MS. Latin 2777) and in many other manuscripts, the document ... is addressed by Constantine to Pope Sylvester (314-35) ... the Emperor makes a present to the Pope and his successors of the Lateran Palace, of Rome and the provinces, districts, and towns of Italy and all the Western regions.[4]

The *Catholic Encyclopedia* continues: 'This document is without doubt a forgery, fabricated somewhere between the years 750 and 850. As early as the fifteenth century its falsity was known and demonstrated.'

Apparently, however, it was still regarded as authentic and mandatory in 1155 when Adrian used it to back up his privilege to Henry II. By reason of the 'Donation of Constantine' Adrian regarded himself as the sovereign Lord of Ireland and all islands.[5]

As for *Laudabiliter* itself, the Latin text of which is given in the *Book of Leinster*, it contains no 'grant of sovereignty' nor 'any intention of ceremonial investiture of Ireland': 'The Laudabiliter does not contain any transfer of sovereign dominion, so that the Pope would remain the lord of Ireland even after Henry had carried out his proposed invasion and ecclesiastical reformation in that island.'[6]

The bull extols Henry's purpose:

> ... to extend the bounds of the church, to proclaim to
> a rude and untaught people the truth of the Christian
> faith, and to root out nurseries of vice from the field of
> the Lord ... So we ... are pleased and willing ... that
> you shall enter that island and do therein what tends to
> the honour of God and the salvation of the people.[7]

Whether there was need for religious reform in Ireland at
the time we shall see later. What we can state here with
some degree of authority is that Henry and his Norman
barons were hardly the most suitable people to bring
about such reform.

It has often been asserted that *Laudabiliter* itself is a
forgery. Both MacGeoghegan[8] and Bishop John Lynch[9] are
of the opinion that it was fabricated to facilitate the conquest of Ireland by Henry.

On the other hand, the eminent Catholic historian, Rev
Dr John Lanigan, maintains that it is an absolutely authentic document.[10] In this he is joined by most modern
historians, even though no original or copy of *Laudabiliter*
has been found in the Vatican archives. There appears to

43 *Thomas Becket confronting his enemies*

be no known original *Laudabiliter*, only copies of purported grants and privileges which have been used, especially by Giraldus, as proof of the existence of an original bull by Pope Adrian. There is little reason to doubt, however, that the texts quoted in the *Book of Leinster* and by Giraldus in *Expugnatio Hibernica* are not genuine.

Although it was apparently granted in 1155, nothing was publicly heard of *Laudabiliter* until 1175, about twenty years later. This lapse may have raised doubts in the minds of many historians, particularly when it was remembered that Henry, by this time, was trying to curry favour with the papacy.

The first public announcement of the bull was made at a synod at Waterford in 1175, when a confirmatory grant from Pope Alexander III was read. In the interim something had happened in England which made it necessary for Henry to appear to be still a pope's man bent on spreading Christianity in the west.

Archbishop Thomas Becket of Canterbury was murdered on the steps of his church by four Norman knights on 29 December 1170. He had been in dispute with Henry for

44 *Thomas Becket parting from Henry II and Louis VII*

some time and, naturally, the king was held responsible for the murder. Henry was threatened with a papal interdict and, to escape the storm, crossed to Ireland in 1171.

A synod of the Irish Church was held at Cashel in 1171-72 when the Irish bishops signified their acceptance of

45 *Assassination of Thomas Becket*

Henry as their overlord. At this synod, although Adrian's bull was not proclaimed, its purport may well have been communicated privately to the Irish clergy and leaders. This would go a long way towards explaining the readiness with which the Irish accepted Henry and why the bishops each gave him a letter confirming to him and his heirs the kingdom of Ireland. At the conclusion of the synod of Cashel, Henry sent reports with envoys to Pope Alexander. He also sought a papal privilege for his actions in Ireland.

He left Ireland on 17 April 1172. The threat of excommunication still hung over his head so he set about purging his guilt and in May he was reconciled with the papacy.

In September of 1172 the pope not only absolved Henry but promulgated three letters on the Irish question. The

first of these letters congratulated him on his Irish achievement; the second, to the kings and princes of Ireland,
praised them for their submission to Henry and exhorted
them to remain faithful to the oaths they had sworn; the
third, to the Irish ecclesiastical authorities, urged them to
do their part in maintaining Henry's newly acquired
position in Ireland.

The synod of Waterford followed in 1175 when,
apparently, *Laudabiliter* was publicly proclaimed for the
first time and was confirmed by a privilege of Pope Alexander III.

Giraldus says, in his *Expugnatio Hibernica*, that Pope
Adrian's bull was read in conjunction with this privilege,
titled 'Quoniam Ea'; the Welshman says the privilege was
granted in response to the letters of the Irish prelates
acknowledging Henry as overlord.

Rev Dr O'Doherty, in a succinct analysis of all the
documents, says the brief of Adrian IV, granted at the request of John of Salisbury in 1155, is the famous *Laudabiliter*. Then there followed the approval of Alexander for
Henry's settlement in Ireland. He adds: 'At a later date –
in 1176 or 1177 – it seems probable that a further brief
regarding Ireland was granted by Rome; but, if so, this
brief is lost. Its place is taken by the 'Quoniam Ea' of
Giraldus, a document which, at the worst, is a sheer
forgery, and at the best a totally inadequate transcript of
the genuine letter.'[11]

And a summing-up by Curtis: 'Whatever, then, we may
think of the so-called 'Bull' of Adrian, there can be no
doubt that the letters and privilege of a later pope conferred the lordship of Ireland upon Henry II.'[12]

Henry, in return for Pope Adrian's commission to
invade Ireland, gave certain pledges to safeguard the
Church's interests. Giraldus outlines them:

> ... the two pledges which (Henry) gave to Pope
> Adrian, when he obtained his permission to invade and

conquer Ireland, and acted most prudently and discreetly for his own interest, and those of his family and people, when he secured the sanction of the highest earthly authority to an enterprise of so much magnitude, and which involved the shedding of Christian blood. One was, that he would raise up the church of God in that country, and cause a penny to be paid to St Peter for every house in Ireland, as is done in England.[13]

Whether Henry succeeded in 'raising up the church of God' in Ireland is a moot point. The second pledge was honoured – and we had, until recently, our annual Peter's Pence collections as a reminder.

If, then, we are to accept that Henry did have papal approval to enter Ireland to enforce religious reform the question immediately arises: Was such reform really necessary?

I can do no better here than to quote Brian O Cuiv on the Church in Ireland at the time:

It is well known that between the introduction of Christianity in the fifth century and the time of Brian Boroime the Church in Ireland had for the most part met the religious needs of the Irish people from within. Though in communion with Rome, it was to a large extent self-governing and self-renewing and, when circumstances required it, self-reforming. When we come to the eleventh century we find that many of the old monasteries founded by the early saints and their followers were still in existence and flourishing, and that they were spread throughout the country. Many of them, as we know, were centres of learning, but they were primarily religious centres and we may suppose that from them and from others of which we know nothing the spiritual welfare of the people was looked after to some extent. Moreover the *Schottenkloster* or Irish monasteries of Ratisbon, Wurzburg, Mainz and other places in Germany remind us that even in the eleventh century Ireland was sending missionary sons abroad, for those German foundations date from this later era when John of Ireland, Marianus Scottus, Marianus of Ratisbon and others were preaching the gospel or leading lives of asceticism in Europe.

We might suppose that with numerous religious houses throughout Ireland and the missionary movement under way again, the moral well-being of the people was assured. Unfortunately this was not so, for after the long centuries of the Viking wars and consequent upheavals, there was spiritual and moral laxity. Deeds of violence were frequent, even against priests and nuns and against church property. The sacraments were neglected, there was a reluctance to pay tithes, and the marriage laws of the Church were disregarded. The laxity about marriage, it is true, may have been due to the brehon laws which differed from the rules of the Church in this regard. However, there was clearly a need for a spiritual renewal, and with it reform of the Church itself, for part of the trouble lay in the organisation, which was monastic rather than diocesan, a feature which resulted in a lack of priests engaged in pastoral work. Another characteristic of the Irish Church was that there was hereditary succession to certain benefices and that these were frequently held by laymen. Of course, to a people accustomed to the principle of hereditary succession in other walks of life, including poetry, this would not have seemed strange.

At any rate reform was needed, and it came. Through the renewed contacts with Western Europe, established by the latest wave of Irish missionaries, and also through Irish pilgrims who found their way to Rome, Irishmen at home became aware of the vast church reform which was taking place on the Continent. The fact that the Norse towns had become Christianised

46 *A Cistercian monk*   47 *Seal of St Anselm*

and from early in the eleventh century looked to
Canterbury for episcopal consecration was an important factor.[14]

After listing the early reformers and their achievements,
from Mael Isa Ua hAinmire, who was consecrated bishop
of Waterford by St Anselm of Canterbury in 1096, down
to Cellach Ua Sinaig, bishop of Armagh and primate of
Ireland, who presided over a national synod near Cashel
in 1111 (when Ireland was divided into twenty-four sees,
replacing the old monastic organisation), Brian O Cuiv
continues:

> Forty years were to pass before reorganisation was
> brought to a successful conclusion. In the meantime a
> younger man, Mael Maedóc, whom we know as St
> Malachy, had succeeded to Cellach and it fell to him to
> conduct the necessary negotiations with the Pope. On
> his journeys to Rome he stayed with St Bernard at
> Clairvaux and he poured forth to him his concern about
> the state of Ireland. He was so impressed with what he
> saw in Clairvaux that he introduced the Cistercians to
> Ireland where their first settlement was begun at

Mellifont in 1142 on land given by the king of Airgialla (Oriel).

This monastery, incidentally, was the one endowed by Dervorgilla and in which she died in 1193.

Brian O Cuiv goes on:

St Malachy died in Clairvaux in 1148 on his second journey to Rome, but his design for the Irish Church bore fruit four years later when, at the Synod of Kells, Ireland was divided into thirty-six sees with four archbishoprics, and the pallia were distributed by the Papal Legate, Cardinal Paparo, to the archbishops of Armagh, Cashel, Dublin and Tuam. So in 1152 the Legate could report to the Pope that the Church in Ireland had now the basic organisation to look to the pastoral care of its flock. The reports which led to Pope Adrian's strange grant to King Henry II three years

48 *Mellifont Abbey*

later were either deliberately false or were based on a misunderstanding of the true state of affairs in Ireland.

The pope, need it be repeated, was English; and Henry had had his eye on Ireland for some time. Dermot MacMurrough, unwittingly perhaps, now became the instrument by which Henry put *Laudabiliter* into effect. Indeed, it is suggested that Dermot, through ecclesiastics or monks, may have known about the bull and the authority which it gave to Henry.[15]

At any rate, when Dermot with his small party of followers left Ireland, on 1 August 1166, he had obviously made up his mind to ask Henry for assistance.

8
Recruiting

MacMurrough had to travel far afield to find King Henry. He landed at Bristol, where he found shelter for a short time with the monks at the priory of St Augustine and made contact with one Robert FitzHarding, a trusted friend of Henry. FitzHarding extended the hospitality of his house to Dermot and briefed him on the king's movements. Then the Wexford man set off to find him, making first for Normandy where Henry was then believed to be.

The Song of Dermot describes MacMurrough's travels in search of Henry:

> *It is well, my lords, that I should tell you*
> *How Dermot goes through Normandy:*
> *To seek King Henry then he goes*
> *Up and down, forwards and back;*
> *He sent messages and made enquiries*
> *Until he found King Henry.*

When Dermot finally caught up with the elusive king it was well into 1167, Henry having spent Christmas 1166 at Poitiers in Aquitaine and then gone further south into Guyenne. Dermot eventually encountered him back in Aquitaine and there the two kings met – the big, corpulent, restless Angevin, and the tall, burly Irishman with the hoarse voice.

MacCarthaigh's Book describes the event:

> The king of England at that time was King Henry,

duke of Normandy, Aquitaine, and Anjou, and lord of Wales and Scotland, according to the books of the Galls. On MacMurchadha's arrival, the king welcomed him and kept him with him for a while and then allowed him to return to England with letters and treasure. As it was not possible for himself or his forces to go with MacMurchadha ... [1]

The last part of the extract undoubtedly refers to the fact that at the time Henry was having trouble with his own subjects in Aquitaine, of which he was duke under the nominal suzerainty of the king of France. It is doubtful if he was able to give Dermot much of his time or attention, although it is recorded that he welcomed the Irishman and listened sympathetically to his tale of how he was wronged and cast out of his kingdom.

Nevertheless, Henry must at this juncture have recollected his turbulent barons – and *Laudabiliter*. After further discussions with Dermot, who swore fealty and allegiance to him, Henry gave him a letter which, in effect, was a permit to recruit volunteers among the Norman colonists in Wales to assist him in regaining his kingdom in Leinster. Perhaps it was not as much as Dermot expected. *The Song of Dermot* probably reflects his disappointment:

> *But the King of England*
> *For Dermot, according to the lay,*
> *Did nothing in truth*
> *Beyond the promise, as people say.*
> *When King Dermot saw*
> *That he could get no aid*
> *From King Henry as he had promised him*
> *He would not stay there any longer.*

Disappointed though he may have been, Dermot nevertheless had his letters patent in which Henry 'gave permission to everyone who wished to go with MacMur-

THE
ANGEVINS

Solway F

York

Dublin

Chester

Wexford
Waterford

Pembroke   Gloucester
Milford   Bristol   London
                Winchester   Canterbury
                Portsmouth

English Channel

Havre
                Normandy

Argentan

Brittany

Poitiers

Dermot's journey to France, 1166/67 ....
Henry II's journey to Ireland, 1171 ————

Aquitaine

Gascony

49 Dermot's journey to France: Henry II's to Ireland

re leuarer: bello pluscm̄ inteſtino
tanqm̄ in ſe coniurant Imodāta
corp' exatōne torquebat. Ram p̄
rer belloꝶ tēpora q̄ frequent' im

50 *Henry II*

chadha to Ireland for the purpose of recovering his territory'.[2]

Giraldus had left us the text of Henry's letter:

> Henry, king of England, duke of Normandy and Aquitaine, and count of Anjou, to all his liegemen, English, Normans, Welsh and Scots, and to all nations subject to his sway, greeting: Whensoever these letters shall come unto you, know that we have received Dermot, prince of Leinster, into our grace and favour; wherefore whosoever within the bounds of our territories shall be willing to give him aid, as our vassal and liegeman, in recovering his dominion, let him be assured of our favour and licence in that behalf.[3]

Armed with this licence Dermot returned to Bristol. But even with Henry's letter he found there was no rush to join his expeditionary force. We can picture him, a commanding figure, surrounded by his Irish followers, reading Henry's letter in the public places in Bristol, stared at by a curious crowd – who listen, shrug their shoulders and pass on.

Yet Dermot, bitter in his determination, continued his quest for volunteers:

> *King Dermot, then you must know*
> *Goes everywhere seeking aid.*
> *Aid everywhere he seeks*
> *In Wales and in England.*
> *So far did he ask for aid*
> *Up and down in this kingdom*
> *That he had an interview,*
> *So says the geste, with Earl Richard.*[4]

Earl Richard was Richard FitzGilbert de Clare, earl of Pembroke, better known to us as Strongbow. To meet him Dermot had crossed the Severn into south Wales, in the knowledge that here surely, among the warring barons, he would find adventurers in plenty to aid him. He had gone to the right place and, in Strongbow, he had found the right man – a veteran of many battles, the representative of an influential Norman family, a man now down on his luck whose estate had been confiscated by Henry. He was thus a likely candidate for any adventure that promised spoils.

Strongbow's family was an illustrious one. His father, Gilbert de Clare, was created earl of Pembroke by Stephen, constable of Cardigan, in 1138, and his grandfather had received the grant of Cardigan from Henry I, seizing it from its Welsh chieftain Cadogan. Gilbert's grandfather, Richard de Clare, had fought at Hastings in 1066 and was descended from Godfrey, a natural son of Richard I of Normandy.

Strongbow himself was between fifty and sixty and a widower at the time, his first wife having been a niece of Hervey de Monte Marisco, one of the first invaders. He seemingly got his nickname from his father. Recording Gilbert's death in 1159 the *Annals of Wales* say: *'Gilbertus comes qui Strangboga dictus est orbit.'* Giraldus describes him as *'Strigulensis Ricardus Gilleberti,'* to which Camden's text adds, *'Dictus Strongbow, fortis arcus.'*[5]

The Geraghty edition of the *Annals of the Four Masters* says: 'Gilbert de Clare, earl of Pembroke, being a famous archer, was designated *de arcu forte* or *Strongbow* and his son Richard also bore that name.'[6]

This, then, was the man to whom Dermot finally turned for aid and the man who, by his agreement with the Leinster king, was to influence many of his kind to flock to MacMurrough's standard.

Strongbow's promise of assistance, however, was not lightly won. Dermot secured his agreement eventually by offering his daughter Aoife in marriage and the prospect of the kingdom of Leinster in succession to Dermot himself: 'Aoife, daughter of MacMurchadha, was to be given in marriage to the earl, and the province of Leinster after MacMurchadha's death, in consideration of his

51 *Chepstow Castle*

coming to Ireland to effect the conquest for MacMurch-adha in the ensuing summer.'[7]

Having succeeded in winning over Strongbow to his cause, Dermot proceeded towards St David's in Pembrokeshire, and sought out Rhys ap Griffith or Gruffudd, the Welsh prince of south Wales, who had as prisoner 'a knight of great renown', Robert FitzStephen. Possibly Strongbow had told Dermot about FitzStephen, who was to become one of the most important men of the whole adventure.

He was a son of the famous Nesta, aunt of Rhys, by Stephen, the constable of Cardigan. According to Giraldus, Robert had been taken prisoner and delivered over to Rhys through the treachery of his men at Aberteivy (Cardigan). Giraldus has this to say about him: '... stout in person, with a handsome countenance, and in stature somewhat above the middle height; he was bountiful, generous, and pleasant, but too fond of wine

52 *Robert FitzStephen*

and women ... An excellent man, the true pattern of singular courage and unparalleled enterprise.'

This obviously likeable character had been three years in prison when Rhys offered him his freedom if he would take up arms against Henry. But Robert was loyal to his king and was reluctant to do this. Just then MacMurrough appeared fortuitously on the scene looking for adventurers and Rhys, at the behest of Robert's half-brothers, David (bishop of St David's) and Maurice FitzGerald, released Robert on condition that he went to Ireland with MacMurrough.

The scribe in *MacCarthaigh's Book* writes:

> MacMurchadha came to an agreement with the king of Wales concerning the help he had promised to send with him to Ireland. The king aided him by giving him Robert FitzStephen, whom he had in prison for three years, and by affirming to MacMurchadha that he would come to Ireland with him in consideration of his release, together with as much of a following as he could get.

Dermot now had Strongbow and Robert FitzStephen on his side – two influential and respected men among the Norman settlers in Wales. Others began to flock to his standard almost immediately. No doubt word of Dermot's speculative grants of land to the would-be invaders spread rapidly. To Maurice FitzGerald and Robert Fitz-Stephen, for instance, Dermot had agreed to give a grant of the town of Wexford and the two adjoining cantreds if they came over to aid him in the following spring.[8] Since a cantred of the land contained one hundred manors or townlands, of 1,000 acres each, the prospects for such land-hungry barons were alluring.

All along the road to St David's Dermot secured further promises of assistance from other Cambro-Norman knights, and in the district of Rhos he enlisted supporters from among the Flemish settlers there.

Things were now looking considerably brighter for Dermot. While awaiting a favourable opportunity to return to Ireland he is pictured by Giraldus as: '...sniffing from the Welsh coast the air of Ireland, wafted on the western breezes and, as it was, inhaling the scent of his beloved country. He had no small consolation feasting his eyes on the sight of his land, though the distance was such that it was difficult to distinguish between the mountains and clouds.'[9]

During his absence Dermot had maintained communication with his followers in Uí Ceinnsealaigh and he felt the time was now opportune for a quiet return to Ferns:

> *To Ireland then he crossed*
> *With as many men as he had.*
> *But Dermot, the noble king,*
> *Did not bring with his warriors*
> *Any Englishmen on this occasion*
> *According to the account of my informant,*
> *Except one Richard, as I have heard say,*
> *A knight of Pembrokeshire,*
> *Richard the son of Godibert,*
> *A knight he was of good parts*
> *Together with knights, archers and sergeants*
> *But I know not up to what number.*
> *For they were not long*
> *In Ireland, these men*
> *For they were hardly able to do any good there*
> *To the king in the land*
> *Because they were only a few men*
> *Who crossed over in haste.*[10]

This small party which accompanied Dermot back to County Wexford in the late summer of 1167 may have been in the nature of a reconnaissance group, sent ahead to assess the chances of an invasion and perhaps locate a suitable landing-place. The group probably consisted of

53 Roch Castle

Normans, Flemings and Welsh, under Richard FitzGodebert, who thus became the very first of the invaders to land in Ireland.

This Richard, the son of Godebert the Fleming, hailed from the district of Rhos in Pembrokeshire where the family had a castle near Haverford. As this castle was built on a rock (French, *roche*) the family became known as FitzGodebert de la Roche. Orpen says both Richard and his brother Robert took the name de la Roche.[11] Of Richard we hear very little more, as he seems to have taken no active part in the subsequent invasion. But from him and his brother Robert, who was later granted a large estate in south Wexford, the widespread families named Roche have descended.[12]

The Irish annalists and Giraldus do not agree entirely on the date of Dermot's return or on the exact sequence of the events that followed. Since the Irish annals generally are fairly reliable as to medieval dates and since they are unanimous as to the important dates in our chronology we may accept, from the *Annals of Inisfallen* and others, that Dermot returned to Ferns in August 1167.

We are told that he 'landed in a place where he had many enemies and few friends'.[13] This place has been identified by historians as Glascarrig, 'a small creek and promontory on the open coast of Wexford, about twelve miles south of Arklow head, and the same distance from Ferns.'[14]

Dermot's landing must have gone unnoticed for he was able to proceed peaceably to Ferns. 'He went secretly to Fearna Mor Maodhog, putting himself under the protection of the clergy and community of Fearna; and he stayed with them sad and wretched during the time that elapsed until the coming of summer,' says Keating. Giraldus agrees with this, saying that Dermot spent the winter in retirement in the monastery at Ferns.

But MacMurrough was not one to waste time, 'sad and wretched' in a monastery, while a kingdom remained to be rewon. Undoubtedly he had little difficulty in recovering power in Uí Ceinnsealaigh, where his brother was nominal king and where his son Donal Cavanagh had been looking after his interests. Dermot's acceptance by the clergy and monks of Ferns, while understandable in view of his munificence, may be taken as an indication of how local opinion had swung back in his favour – if indeed it had ever swung away.

Although the annals state that he returned 'with a force of Galls' and took the kingdom of Uí Ceinnsealaigh, the process of re-establishing himself was probably much more gradual.[15] With his own principality again under his control, Dermot reasserted his claim to his lost kingdom of Leinster. News of this development was not long in reaching the ears of High-King Ruairi O'Connor. Calling up Dermot's old enemy Tiernan O'Rourke, Ruairi marched against Dermot and defeated him in a battle at Cill Osnadh (now Kellistown), a few miles south-east of Carlow town.

Twenty-five of Dermot's men, including a Welshman who may have been a son of Rhys ap Griffith, were killed in this encounter. Dermot gave hostages – among them two of his sons – to Ruairi in return for which (and a promise to behave himself in future, no doubt) the high-king allowed him to retain ten cantreds of Uí Ceinnsealaigh, on condition that he recognised the high-king-ship of O'Connor and foreswore his claim on the kingdom of Leinster. Of greater interest is the fact that Ruairi ordered Dermot to pay a hundred ounces of gold to O'Rourke in reparation for the 'abduction' of his wife Dervorgilla.

It may have been *after* these setbacks that Dermot retired to the monastery in Ferns, to brood and plot anew, and it may have been then also that he sent Richard FitzGodebert and his men back to Wales. It cannot be said with certainty, however, that they all returned. A few of the knights may have stayed behind in Uí Ceinnsealaigh to act as 'fifth columnists', to plan for the coming invasion and to keep their comrades in Wales informed of events in Ireland.

The stage was now set for the actual invasion.

9
Preparation

Meanwhile, back in Pembrokeshire, preparations for the invasion went ahead; the genius of the Normans for military organisation was undoubtedly put to good effect in planning and forming assault parties, in plotting sea courses and landing-places, in commissioning ships, horses, arms and armour, and provisions.

Curtis writes:

When it came to the art of war and fortification, the superiority of the Normans had been displayed already in England, south Italy and Palestine. The 'miles' or mounted soldier of gentle blood wore a mail shirt covering his body, thighs and arms, and a conical iron helmet, with a guard for the nose and a chain covering for the neck and throat. Their horses were light coursers which had no armoured protection. A much more

54 *Norman arms and armour*

elaborate plate armour for man and horse was to become fashionable by 1200, but the equipment of the Geraldines and their companions proved the right thing for Irish war and lingered for many generations … The Irish Gael, though given to war and with plenty of natural courage, for the most part fought in linen tunics with light axes, swords and spears. To the Irish kings a battle was intended to achieve an immediate object; that achieved, their armies retired. To the Norman-French, war was a business proposition and their enterprise a joint-stock company out of which profits were expected. A battle once gained, the next step was to throw up an impregnable castle, the next was to organise the conquered country into a manor or barony and seek if necessary a charter for it from earl or king.[1]

In the Norman armies there were three main military groups – the knights, the men-at-arms, and the archers. The knights, those who were conferred with this order of chivalry, usually fought in armour on horseback, armed with long lances and shields. The men-at-arms were landed gentry and relations of knights and were often called esquires. They also wore armour, and carried swords and shields. Many of these landed gentry also

55 Irish fighters

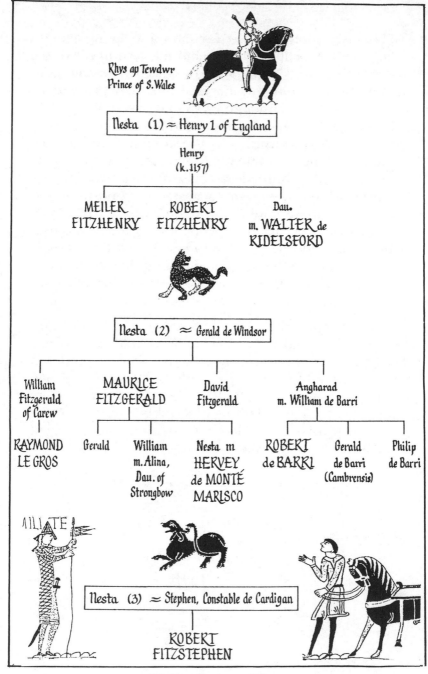

56 *Family tree of Nesta*

fought from horseback and all were self-equipped. The archers also fought on foot, were lightly armoured for mobility and carried the deadly cross-bow, whose iron-tipped arrows could transfix a man at several hundred yards.

Such were the men: who were their leaders? As we have seen, Strongbow, Robert FitzStephen and Maurice FitzGerald were among the first to answer Dermot's recruiting call. In fact most of the first invaders were blood relations, having a common progenitor in the beautiful Nesta.

Princess Nesta, whom we met briefly in an earlier chapter, was daughter of Rhys ap Tewdwr, prince of south Wales, who fought for his country against Henry I. She was taken as a hostage by Henry who made her his mistress and gave her a son, also named Henry, who was killed in 1157. This Henry had two sons, Meiler and Robert FitzHenry, both of whom were among the first invaders.

The remarkable Nesta, described as 'the most beautiful woman in Wales', next married Gerald de Windsor, constable of Pembroke, by whom she had three sons – William FitzGerald of Carew (who died in 1173), Maurice FitzGerald, the invader, and David FitzGerald, bishop of St David's (who both died in 1176). She also had, by Gerald, a daughter named Angharad who married William de Barri of Manorbier. There were three sons of that marriage: our chronicler Giraldus Cambrensis, Robert, who was among the invaders, and Philip, who got large estates in Cork.

Finally Nesta married or was mistress of Stephen, constable of Cardigan, by whom she bore Robert Fitz-Stephen. Thus the FitzGeralds, the FitzHenrys, the Barrys and FitzStephens were all blood relations.

Nor did her progeny among the invaders end there. One of her grandsons was Raymond le Gros (son of William FitzGerald of Carew). Two others (the sons of

Maurice Fitzgerald) were Gerald and William (who married Alina, daughter of Strongbow). Her granddaughter, also named Nesta, married Hervey de Monte Marisco, who was Strongbow's uncle.

On the FitzHenry side, Meiler obtained lands in Kildare, and his sister married one of the first invaders, Walter de Ridelsford.

Small wonder that Wright noted that 'the first conquerors of Ireland were nearly all descendants of Nesta, either by her two husbands or through the son she had by Henry I of England'.[2] From Gerald of Windsor and Nesta are descended, then, the great families which made such an indelible mark on later Irish history – the Fitz-Geralds of Kildare and Desmond, the Carews, Fitz-Maurices, Gerards, Barrys and Graces (as the descendants of Raymond le Gros became known).

Other Norman family names prominent among the early invaders were Talbot (from the barony of that name near Rouen), Devereux or D'Evereux (also from near Rouen), Rochfort (now Rochford), Neville, Browne, Poer (now Power, pronounced Poor in south Wexford).

To Pembrokeshire may be traced the families of Barry, Bryan, Barrett, Carew, Caunteton (now Condon), Hay, Keating, Mayler, Roche, Russell, Stackpoole, Scurlock and Walsh.

From Devonshire came Furlong, Bellew, Codd, Cruys (now Cruise) and Hore. Of uncertain origin are Harper or Harpur (said to be descended from Strongbow's harper), Sutton, Stafford, Rossiter, Loundres, Esmonde, French (or ffrench as it is spelled in south Wexford today), Lamport (now Lambert), Peppard, St. John and Turner.

Flemish names prominent among the settlers were Fleming itself (they became barons of Slane), Prendergast (shortened to Pender at times), Chievres (now Cheevers or Chivers), Synad (now Sinnott), Cullin (now Cullen), Wadding, Whythay (now Whitty), Cusac (now Cusack), Siggin (Siggins, pronounced in south Wexford Siggeen),

57 *Norman crusaders*

Boscher (Busher), Parle, Waddick, Bolger, Colfer and Connick.[3]

A survey of these names and a comparison with electoral lists of districts in south Wexford show how resolutely the descendants of the early invaders have remained in the areas where their adventurous ancestors first settled.

'Perhaps in no county in Ireland,' comments Gabriel O'C. Redmond, 'can there be found so many who trace their descent in a direct line from the triumphant knights of the reign of Henry II.'[4]

Camden lists the 'persons who came with Dermot MacMorrog into Ireland' as follows:

> Richard Strongbow, Earle of Pembroch, who by Eve the daughter of Morrog the Irish petie king aforesaid, had one only, and who brought unto William Mareschall the title of the Earledome of Pembroch, with faire lands in Ireland, and a goodly issue, five sonnes, who succeeded one another in a row, all childless; and as many daughters, which enriched their husbands, Hugh Bigod, Earle of Norfolke; Guarin Mont-chenfey, Gilbert Clare, Earle of Gloucester, William Ferrars, Earle of Derby and William Breofe, with children, honors and possessions. Robert Fitz-Stephen, Harvey de Montmarish, Maurice Prendergast, Robert Barr, Meiler Meilerine, Maurice Fitz-Gerald, Redmund nephew of Fitz-Stephen, William Ferrand, Miles de Cogan, Gualter de Ridensford, Gualter and Alexander sonnes of Maurice Fitz-Gerald, William Notte, Robert Fitz-Bernard, Hugh Lacie, William Fitz-Aldelm, William Macarell, Hemphrey Bohun, Hugh de Gundevill, Philip de Hasting, Hugh Tirell, David Walsh, Robert Poer, Osbert de Herloter, William de Bendenges, Adam de Gernez, Philip de Breos, Griffin nephew of Fitz-Stephen, Raulfe Fitz-Stephen, Walter de Barry, Philip Walsh, Adam de Hereford. To whom may be added out of Giraldus

Cambrensis, John Courcy, Hugh Contilon, Redmund Fitz-Hugh, Miles of St David's, and others.[5]

'The first feudal band to invade Ireland, Maurice Fitz-Gerald and the rest,' comments Curtis, 'were a family party, putting their stock into a common enterprise and ready for the great jump-over into Ireland.'

These, then, were the men poised for the invasion, the men to whom Dermot, from his refuge in the Augustinian monastery at Ferns, now sent word that the time was opportune. *The Song of Dermot* takes up the story:

> *(He) then sent word*
> *By letter and by messenger*
> *He sent over Morice Regan*
> *His own interpreter*
> *To Wales this man crossed over.*
> *The letters of King Dermot*
> *Which the king sent in all directions*
> *To earls, barons, knights,*
> *Squires, sergeants, common soldiers,*
> *Horsemen and foot*
> *In all directions the king sent word.*

The letters which Dermot sent were probably copies of Henry's letters patent and he accompanied these, as *The Song of Dermot* tells us, with new promises of riches and rewards to all who might come to his aid.

This time the Normans were ready. All they awaited now was the spring and a fair wind for the shores of Ireland.

10
Invasion

Thus does *MacCarthaigh's Book* baldly describe the most significant event in Irish history for a thousand years: 'Robert FitzStephen came to Ireland, as he had promised MacMurchadha, with thirty knights, three score esquires, and three hundred archers. They made port at Banabh, and leaving their ships, encamped at the harbour until MacMurchadha arrived with five hundred supporters,' an account supported by Giraldus: 'FitzStephen ... had mustered thirty men-at-arms, of his own kindred and retainers, together with sixty men in half-armour, and about 300 archers and foot-soldiers, the flower of the youth of Wales, and embarking them in three ships, landed at the Banne.'

The *Annals of the Four Masters* is cryptic: 'The fleet of the Flemings came from England in the army of MacMurchadha to contest the kingdom of Leinster for him; they were seventy heroes dressed in coats of mail ...' and we

58 *Carrying hauberks to the ships*

must turn to *The Song of Dermot* for a little more detail:

> Then Robert the son of Stephen
> Got himself ready the first ...
> Brave knights of great renown
> He brought with him, nine or ten.
> One was Meiler, the son of Henry
> Who was very powerful;
> And Miles came there also
> The son of the bishop of St David's
> Knights came there and barons
> Whose names for the most part I do not know.
> There crossed over a baron
> With seven companions
> Maurice de Prendergast was his name
> As the song tells us.
> Hervey too, in truth, crossed over,
> He was of Mount-Maurice.
> About three hundred crossed over
> Knights and common folk besides.
> At Bannow they landed
> With all their men
> When they had landed
> And had all disembarked
> They made their men encamp
> On the seashore.

ISTI PORTANT:ARMAS: ADNAVES: EThIC TRAhVNT: CARRVM CVMVINO:ETARMIS:

59 ... *and provisions*

But what drama is hidden in the bald words of the Irish annals and Giraldus and in the poetic narrative of *The Song of Dermot!*

The Normans and their Flemish and Welsh comrades had embarked at Milford Haven, their horses prancing aboard the ships, the shouts of command and farewell in French, Flemish and Welsh echoing across the water. Pennants fluttered from the long lances of the knights and the sunlight glinted on armour and shield.

The Normans, like the Welsh, were skilled seamen, an inheritance from their Norse ancestors. Their ships, too, had inherited many of their features from the Norse *snorrs* of old – they were long, open, and had one mast on which was hoisted a square sail. They depended also on oars, long sweeps each pulled by two men, and they were steered by a large oar on the starboard side near the stern. The shields of the warriors hung along the bulwarks as a protection for the rowers. Each ship was capable of carrying about 120 men with some horses and provisions.

The first assault party under FitzStephen embarked in three ships, moved easily down the enclosed haven at Milford, then rounding St Anne's Head, met the first surges of the turbulent channel that stretched between them and the Wexford coast.[1] Out between the little islands of Skokholm to the south and Skomer to the north, the long ships moved, gradually leaving the Welsh coast

60 *Arriving to embark, boarding*

behind. Soon it sank below the horizon.

Not for long are they out of sight of land, however, for within hours the distant peak of what is now called Mount Leinster, far inland, juts above the western horizon. But there is still a long pull before land is reached.

FitzStephen keeps his fleet a little further south than might be thought correct but he wishes to avoid Norse shipping from the port of Wexford.

Gabriel O'C. Redmond writes:

> Robert FitzStephen was well aware that the Danish stronghold at Wexford was impregnable by sea. When he approached the coast of Ireland with his small band of mail-clad knights and archers, he wisely and prudently war-hawked the sable Raven, emblem of the fierce Dubhgoill, and steering his troopships in a south-westerly direction he rounded Carnsore Point, directed their course towards the Peninsula of Hook and effected a safe and unopposed disembarkation at *la Banue*, now Bannow, on the 1st May, 1169.[2]

We are not certain that the first landing took place on 1 May. Giraldus says the event took place *'circa* Kalendas Maii' (about the Kalends of May) which might be either the day before the Kalends, 30 April, or the day after, 2 May.[3]

As the Welsh historian does not give the exact day of

61 ... *and sailing*

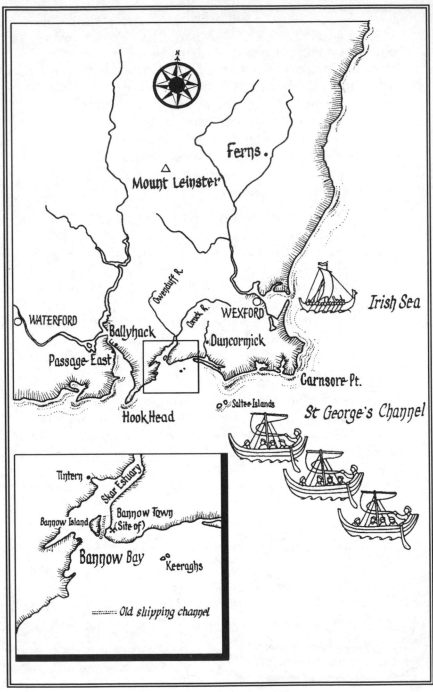

62 Map of Wales and Ireland

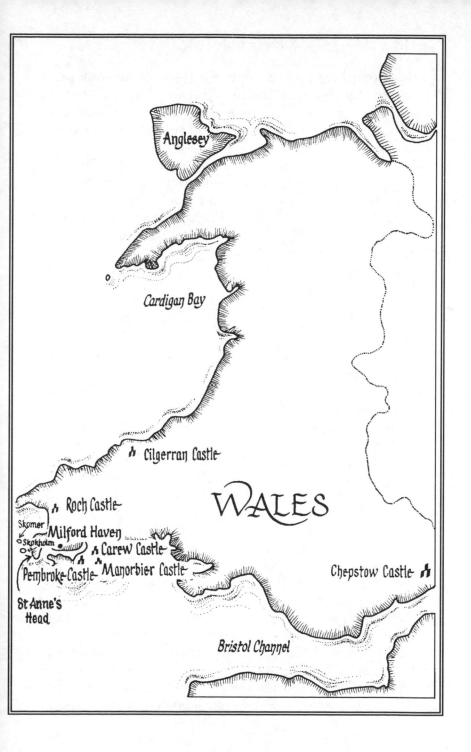

Anglesey

Cardigan Bay

Cilgerran Castle

WALES

Roch Castle

Skomer
Skokholm
Milford Haven

Carew Castle

Pembroke Castle
Manorbier Castle

Chepstow Castle

St Anne's
Head

Bristol Channel

the month, we must accept that the landing took place within the first week or ten days of May, and that the invaders may have had to remain on Bannow Island for some days until the return of a messenger sent to Dermot in Ferns.

If there is some disagreement about the date of the first landing, there should be none about its location. *The Song of Dermot* says it took place *'à la Banne'* (Orpen thinks this should read *à la Banue*). Giraldus says *'apud Banuam'* (near or at Bannow). There can be little doubt that both accounts refer to Bannow.[4]

In an early deed relating to the granting of lands by Hervey de Monte Marisco to Christ Church, Canterbury, mention is made of *insula de Banewe* (the island of Bannow) and it is, in my opinion, possible that *Banewe* is partly Norse in origin, *ee* or *eye* meaning 'island'.[5]

There were several good reasons why FitzStephen should have chosen Bannow as his beach-head. It was one of the few safe anchorages on the south coast of Wexford, in MacMurrough's territory of Uí Ceinnsealaigh yet far enough from the Norse strongholds of Wexford and Waterford to permit an unresisted landing. The local chieftains, O'Duggan and O'Larkin, were favourable to Dermot and could be counted on not to oppose his allies. It was the nearest safe port to Wales, and furthest from Dermot's other enemies, O'Connor and O'Rourke. The island of Bannow, on which camp was set up, afforded a measure of defence, and the inhabitants of the fishing village of Bannow, on the mainland, were unlikely to resist the invaders. We may be quite sure that Bannow had been carefully chosen well in advance, probably on the recommendation of both Dermot and the first Flemish reconnaissance party.

Rev James Graves, an eminent nineteenth-century historian, in a paper on 'The Bay and Town of Bannow' refers to the delusiveness of the bay in his time and says the only expanse of deep water adjoined Bannow Island.

But he adds: 'It cannot then be assuming too much to suppose that, at the period of the Anglo-Norman invasion in the reign of Henry II, Bannow Bay was counted a safe harbour, and known as such, amongst the mariners of the opposite English coast.'[6]

In those days, however, Bannow Island really was an island, round which the waters of the Owenduff and Corock rivers divided and flowed into Bannow Bay. The navigable channel then ran on the eastern side of the island and was open to ships up to the year 1657, if not afterwards.

At what period it first silted up and became unusable by shipping we cannot be certain. Writing in 1684 Robert Leigh, of nearby Rosegarland, says the estuary 'was a place of great trade in the times passed ... until the sand filled up the ancient passage near the towne of Bannow'.[7] The shipping channel is still shown on a map of Bannow parish prepared under the Down Survey (1657), So that between then and the time at which Robert Leigh wrote it must have silted up and fallen into disuse. Occasionally since then, violent storms and unusually high tides have sent the waters of the bay swirling back along the original watercourse, encroaching from both north and south and meeting over the low-lying sandy isthmus that joins the island to the mainland. In 1848, for instance, a local historian recorded that he saw the bed of the old channel which was thirty feet deep in places.[8] Even more recently, within living memory in fact, storm-driven tides have washed across the isthmus, recreating the historic island once again.

At any rate we can assume that when the first invaders under FitzStephen ran their ships aground at Bannow, it was probably at a spot well up the channel where, to the west of a knob called Clare Island, there was a large sheltered pool under the only cliffs on Bannow Island.[9] A declivity led up from the beach and, above it, on the cliff-top, was a natural site for a camp.

Here then FitzStephen probably ran his three ships ashore – under the wondering gaze of the villagers on the high ground of the mainland across the channel.[10] Here, on the island, he erected his camp, sent a messenger to Dermot and settled down uneasily while he awaited reinforcements.

Giraldus says the invaders found themselves in a position far from secure 'when the news of their landing was spread abroad'. Even though FitzStephen's little army included 'the flower of the youth of Wales', it was still only about 390 strong, and the Norse of Wexford and Waterford were but half a day's sailing-time away.

The Song of Dermot takes up the story:

> *The English folk sent word*
> *To King Dermot by messenger*
> *That at Bannow with three ships*
> *They had (by then) landed,*
> *And that the king should speedily*
> *Come there without delay.*
> *King Dermot by the direct road*
> *Towards Bannow, next morning*
> *Set out very joyfully*
> *To see the English folk.*

Dermot actually sent his natural son, Donal Cavanagh, ahead of him to make contact with the Normans and he

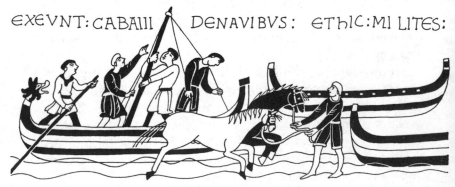

63 *The Normans land*

himself, hastily mustering his followers, followed with 500 men.

Meanwhile FitzStephen's group on Bannow Island had been reinforced. Giraldus tells us that, on the day following the first landing, 'Maurice de Prendergast, a stout and brave soldier, from the district of Ros in south Wales, followed FitzStephen, and having embarked at the port of Milford, with ten men-at-arms, and a large body of archers, in two ships, landed also at the Banne.' This was the second landing.

We may assume that about 200 men arrived under de Prendergast. The forces encamped on Bannow Island now numbered about 600 – and Dermot and his 500 men were on their way. They soon arrived. *The Song of Dermot* resumes:

> *When the king had come*
> *To Bannow to his liegemen*
> *One by one he kissed them*
> *And courteously saluted them.*
> *That night they tarried*
> *On the shore where they were;*
> *But the king on the morrow*
> *Towards Wexford directly*
> *Went immediately, i' faith*
> *To attack the town.*

64 ... *and forage for provisions*

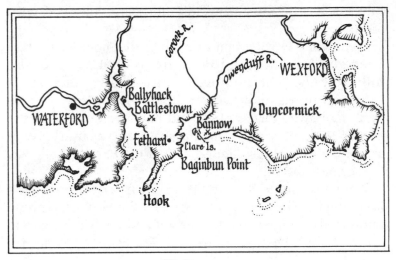

65 *Bannow*

Dermot and the Normans 'confirmed their agreement', says the chronicler in *MacCarthaigh's Book*, 'and unfurling their banners they proceeded with one accord to attack Wexford . . .'

On their way to Wexford, about twenty miles distant, the combined forces, according to tradition, encountered the first opposition of the invasion. At a place now known as Duncormick they had to fight their way across the river which flows past the place. The opposition possibly came from Norse-Irish settled on the tidal inlet, and was quickly overcome.

To commemorate this, the first pitched battle which the invaders had to fight and in which there may have been Norman casualties, a memorial cross is said to have been erected later at the spot.

Philip H. Hore, the Wexford historian, says that in ancient charters the name of the place is rendered 'Croscormuck'.[11] He compares the case of Dundonnell, the old name for Baginbun, which became known as Crosdonenold or Crossdonnell, the reason being that 'a cross was probably erected there to commemorate the pitched battle

66 William FitzAudelin and Meiler FitzHenry

between the invaders (the Normans) and the native Irish'.
In similar manner the old name of Duncormack (Dun
Chormaic) was changed to Croscormuck, after a cross had
been erected to commemorate a battle in this place. Later
the old form, Dun Chormaic, gradually crept back into
use.

Gabriel O'C. Redmond supports this theory: '... the
combined troops of the different races, amounting in all to
960 men, marched to the attack of the town of Wexford,
distant about twenty miles from the Banne. A tradition
which still survives in the neighbourhood says that they
were assailed on the way by a party of the native popula-
tion who were defeated and dispersed.'[12]

The custom of erecting memorial crosses at battle sites
was a long-standing one with the Normans. The earliest
most noteworthy example was the erection of a huge
wooden cross at the Pass of Roncevalles in the Pyrenees
where, in AD 777, 25,000 men of Charlemagne's Frankish
army were killed by the Basques while withdrawing from
Spain.[13]

The skirmish at Duncormick, for that is all it may have
been, deserves greater respect in history than it has got.
This was the first battle of the Norman invasion, the first
attempt to stop the foreigners, the first bloody encounter
in a struggle which was to last for over eight hundred
years.

11
Attack

The town of Wexford in 1169 was a Norse seaport, built around the deep pool of Weisfiord (now the silted-up Crescent) and defended on the landward side by high earthworks and wooden guard-towers. Within the wall dwelt the Norse seafarers, merchants and traders in their timber houses. For more than a century they had been Christians and the town was well served by no fewer than eight churches: three intramural (St Dulogue's, St Mary's and St Patrick's), and five outside the wall, each sited immediately outside one of the five gates of the town (St Michael's, St Bride's, St Peter's, St John and St Brigid – the present Friary – and St Ibar's). The fact that these five churches stood outside the wall, and that three of them were dedicated to Celtic saints, points to the probability that they were built during the period when the Norse were being christianised, and that they were not wholly welcome within the then pagan town. Round these extramural churches were the rude dwellings of the native Irish who worked for and traded with the Norse citizens of Wexford.[1] Being outside the wall these dwellings were first to suffer when the Normans attacked the town.

The Norsemen, evidently appraised of the approach of Dermot's army but not knowing of its foreign complement, decided to give battle outside the walls. They may have believed that this was just another of those ragged Irish assaults in which foot-soldiers, without armour, attacked in disorganised array with spears, battle-axes,

67 The Normans line up

swords and slings. With such a rabble, no matter how courageous, the armoured Norsemen could fairly easily deal.

Picture their shock, then, when faced with the battle ranks of the mailed men-at-arms, the deadly archers and the flanking squadrons of mounted knights and esquires, their long lances poised for the charge, their helmets, shields and armour glinting menacingly as they advanced.

Giraldus describes the scene:

> The people of the town ... were so confident in their good fortune, having been hitherto independent, that they sallied forth, to the number of about 2,000 men,

69 The horsemen charge

68 ... and advance into battle

and meeting the enemy near their camp, resolved on giving them battle. But when they perceived the troops to which they were opposed, arrayed in a manner they had never before witnessed, and a body of horsemen, with their bright armour, helmets and shields, they adopted new plans with a new state of affairs, and having set fire to and burnt the suburbs, forthwith retired within their walls.[2]

A reconstruction of the first Norman assault has been worked out imaginatively by Dr Hadden. The Normans, he wrote:

... had forded the Bishopswater at Slippery Green and come down along the rim of the valley to Bride's

70 ... supported by foot archers

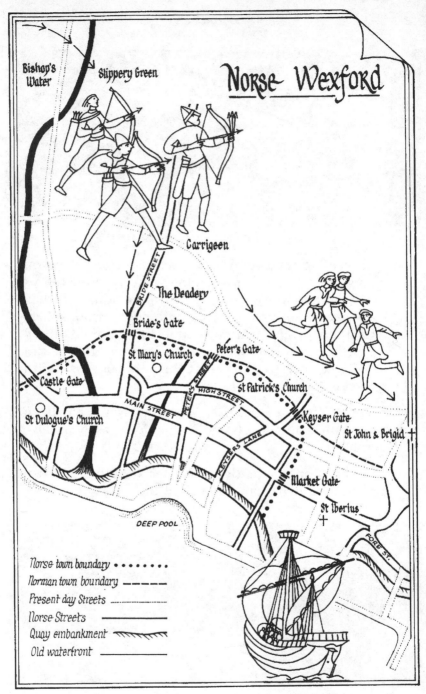

71 Wexford town and the Norman attack

Gate. They found it closed against them and prepared to take the town by storm. FitzStephen deployed his archers along the rocky ridge of Carrigeen, where Roche's Terrace now stands, facing the Danish wall across the wasteland of the Deadery, at a range of a hundred yards. Then he sent in his men-at-arms, covered by dropping flights of arrows, to fill in the ditch and attempt the wall by escalade. But they were decisively repulsed, and FitzStephen broke off the engagement.[3]

The account given by Giraldus fills in the detail:

> FitzStephen lost no time in preparing for the attack; and lining the trenches with those of his troops who wore armour, while the archers were posted so as to command the advanced towers, an assault was made on the walls with loud cries and desperate vigour. But the townsmen were ready to stand on their defence, and casting down from the battlements large stones and beams, repulsed the attack for a while, and caused numerous losses.

The Song of Dermot gives a little more information about the casualties:

> *At this attack the rich king (Dermot)*
> *Lost eighteen of his English;*
> *While the traitors at this time*
> *Lost of their men only three.*
> *All day while it was light*
> *The attack thus lasted*
> *Until it became late*
> *And the men departed.*
> *The men of Dermot the renowned*
> *To their tents returned.*

Giraldus says that his elder brother, Robert de Barri, was among the wounded:

A young soldier, inflamed with ardent valour and dauntless in the face of death, was among the first who scaled the walls; but being struck upon his helmet by a great stone, and falling headlong into the ditch below, narrowly escaped with his life, his comrades with some difficulty drawing him out. Sixteen years afterwards all his jaw-teeth fell out from the effects of this stroke and, what is more strange, new teeth grew in their places.

Here we can justifiably imagine the elder brother, a veteran of the wars, recounting his adventures to Giraldus in Dublin on the latter's visit there with Prince John in 1185 – and perhaps finding a neat explanation for the belated arrival of his wisdom teeth! Undoubtedly it was from Robert that Gerald heard the story of the assault on the walls of Wexford. Giraldus also describes another incident which illustrates the daring of the young Norman soldiers. He writes:

Upon this repulse, withdrawing from the walls, they gathered in haste on the neighbouring strand, and forthwith set fire to all the ships they found lying there. Among these, a merchant ship, lately arrived from the coast of Britain with a cargo of corn and wine, was moored in the harbour; and a band of the boldest youths rowing out in boats got on board the vessel but were carried out to sea, the sailors having cut the hawsers from the anchors, and the wind blowing from the west; so that it was not without great risk and hard rowing, after taking to their boats again, that they regained the land.

The Norman youths may have hoped to capture the valuable corn and wine on the vessel, as ample provisions were very necessary to the army of the invaders, and they were not certain of supplies from Wales. However, that tantalising cargo of corn and wine eluded them, the merchant ship standing off or sailing away, and the disappointed youths returned to camp for the night.

On the following morning (Tuesday), 'after Mass had been celebrated throughout the army', the attack on the town was renewed. But the Norsemen had had enough. Giraldus continues:

> When they (the Normans) drew near the walls, the townsmen, despairing of being able to defend them, and reflecting that they were disloyally resisting their prince, sent envoys to Dermot commissioned to treat of the terms of peace. At length, by the mediation of two bishops, who chanced to be in the town at that time, and other worthy and peaceable men, peace was restored, the townsmen submitting to Dermot, and delivering four of their chief men as hostages for their fealty to him.

We are not told who the bishops were who chanced to be in the town at the time, but it is believed they were the bishops of Ossory and Ferns. Dr Hadden says that the peace negotiations were concluded through the bishop of Ferns, then resident in Wexford.[4] At any rate the Norsemen acknowledged Dermot as their overlord and agreed to aid him in his bid to regain the kingship of Leinster.

Dermot, to reward his foreign allies and to fulfil his promises of land, granted the town and 'the whole territory appertaining to it' (the cantred of the Ostmen as it was called) to FitzStephen and FitzGerald. *MacCarthaigh's Book* says that after the capture of Wexford: 'MacMurchadha, as he had promised, handed it over to Robert FitzStephen and Maurice FitzGerald, together with the country to the east and the west of it.' (FitzGerald, it should be noted, had not yet arrived in Ireland.)

To Hervey de Monte Marisco, the uncle of Strongbow, Dermot granted two cantreds of land lying between the towns of Wexford and Waterford, to hold to him and his heirs in fee. This area, corresponding roughly to the present-day barony of Bargy with parts of Forth and Shelburne and comprising 200,000 acres, must have seemed an unbelievable reward to Hervey, 'a man of fallen fortunes, having neither armour nor money', who had been sent to Ireland by Strongbow merely to inquire into its resources and report back to his nephew in Wales. Other Norman and Flemish knights and esquires also obtained grants of lands. Dr Gabriel O'C. Redmond comments: 'The feudal or subordinate military policy was so thoroughly adopted in the Wexford land tenures, as to warrant the idea that each original officer of the invading force obtained a fee of land as his pay, and for future services.'[5]

These initial grants marked the start of the intensive Norman and Flemish colonisation of the southern baronies of County Wexford – a colonisation which resulted in the singular characteristics noted in the inhabitants of the area down to the present day.

Wexford town, now in the hands of the Normans, was no longer the prosperous trading port and bailiwick of the Norsemen only. Henceforth its trade was to pass into Norman hands, with the result that the rich Norse merchants appear to have gradually retired to their estates in the barony of Forth. According to Dr Hadden an official census taken a hundred years later showed a small community of them still resident there.

Dermot, having made his land grants, returned to Ferns. *The Song of Dermot* says:

> *Thence Dermot set out*
> *Towards Ferns, as soon as he could*
> *In order to heal his wounded*
> *And to rest his barons.*

It is recorded that for three weeks he and his barons feasted and celebrated; then they got down to the serious business of planning the next moves in the campaign. The position of the invaders, even with the capture of Wex-

72 *Preparing food*

ford, was far from secure. Their bridgehead in south Wexford was vulnerable to attack from the north and west; as yet there had been no time to erect fortifications at key points on its perimeter. Dermot and his small army stood between them and the greater forces of High-King Ruairi, but Dermot, even at the height of his power, was no match for the combined forces of O'Connor, O'Rourke and other Irish subkings.

Following the old military maxim that attack is the best form of defence, the Normans and Dermot decided at their conferences in Ferns to do just that. They marched first against Ossory.

73 . . . *and serving the feast*

12
Counter-Moves

The kingdom of Ossory, at the time of the Norman invasion, comprised most of the present County Kilkenny and part of Laoighis. The area had formerly been part of the territory of Leinster under Dermot's overlordship, which may have been one reason why MacMurrough and his allies now marched against it over the Blackstairs mountains.

A second reason may have been that Dermot's eldest son Eanna, held captive by King Donal MacGiolla Phadraig since 1167, had been blinded by his captor. Thus revenge motivated Dermot in his decision to attack Ossory. His army, composed of Irish, Normans, Flemings, Welsh and Norse, the latter unenthusiastic allies, now numbered at least 2,000 men and all (except the Norse) were in good fighting spirit. But MacGiolla Phadraig, besides being Dermot's bitter foe, was also a stout warrior. Dermot knew his mettle and forewarned his allies of the likelihood of a stiff resistance.

The battle which ensued was a long and fiercely fought encounter. MacGiolla Phadraig, Giraldus tells us, made the most of the thick woods and numerous bogs through which the invaders had to pass. Eventually, towards the close of day, the Ossorians were driven into the open where the Norman cavalry pursued and cut them down.

According to *MacCarthaigh's Book*, Dermot 'inflicted slaughter and took hostages from MacGiolla Phadraig as an earnest of submission to him'. Giraldus says that 200 Irish were killed on the Ossorian side; their heads were

134

cut off and laid at Dermot's feet.

The Welsh chronicler then relates an incident so horrible that the reader will be forgiven a shudder of disbelief. Dermot examined the heads, turning them over one by one. 'Among them,' writes Giraldus, 'was the head of one he mortally hated, and taking it by the ears and hair he tore the nostrils and lips with his teeth.' Charles B. Gibson surmises that it might have been the head of the man whom MacGiolla Phadraig had employed to blind Eanna, adding:

> This seems almost too horrible for belief, but an English knight, Castide, who had been taken prisoner by an Irish chieftain, with whom he lived for several years, told Froissart, the historian, that the Irish 'did not consider their enemies dead till they had cut their throats, like sheep, and opened them, and taken away their hearts, which they carry off with them, and which, some say, who are well acquainted with their manners, they devour as delicious morsels'.[1]

Ua Clerigh says the story told by Giraldus is not confirmed by any other historian, adding that 'the credulous author' (Giraldus) was the same man who 'saw with his own eyes' embryo barnacle geese growing like limpets on the rocks along the Irish coast![2]

Goddard Orpen is not so inclined to dismiss the story as a complete fabrication:

> ... this action of Dermot may perhaps indicate the late survival in Ireland of a once widespread superstition noticed by Dr J. G. Fraser (*Psyche's Task*, pages 56-8), viz. 'that one way of allaying the avenging ghost of a murdered man was to taste the blood of the slain, and so, by making him part of oneself, and establishing in the strictest sense a blood-covenant with him, one could convert him from an enemy into an ally ... An historic example from Italy, which at any rate offers

analogies to Dermot's action, occurred at the massacre of the Baglioni in Perugia in 1500, when one of the noble murderers tore from a great wound in his victim's side the still quivering heart, into which he drove his teeth with savage fury.'[3]

With the approach of darkness, Dermot's army encamped for the night in an old dún, planning to pursue the remainder of the Ossorian army on the morrow.

Giraldus describes what happened next:

> The same night, there appeared a strange apparition, first discovered by Randolph FitzRalph, captain of the watch; which was, as he conceived, an army of men well armed. Both he and others conceived it to have been the enemy, concluding in their hearts that the men of Wexford had betrayed them. Randolph ran towards the camp to give the alarm. The sentinel, seeing him coming from where this conceived army stood and taking him for an enemy, gave him, with sword, such a sound blow on the back that he was enforced to touch the ground with his knee. Not long after this, the apparition vanished.

What this 'apparition' was we can only surmise. A figment of the imagination of a jittery captain of the watch, perhaps, easily conjured up in the mist-wreathed woods of a strange land, where wraith-like Ossorian scouts flitted silently around the perimeter of the invaders' camp. Or, as Charles B. Gibson suggests, 'one of those remarkable phenomena which are now and then produced by the excessive refraction of the rays of light'.[4]

Goddard Orpen gives what, to me, sounds like the most likely explanation. He writes:

> Knowing the belief that Irish peasants in the more backward parts have to this day in fairy hosts, and how they associate them and their hostings with the old forts or raths that dot the land, we may shrewdly

74 An Irish rath

suspect that some of Dermot's followers, imbued with the same superstitious beliefs, saw the fairy hosts issue from the old rath in which the army slept, and that from them the panic spread to the rest of the troops.[5]

The site of the rath where the 'apparition' appeared has been located at Dinn Righ, a quarter of a mile south of Leighlin.

Whatever it was that disturbed the troops of Dermot and FitzStephen that night apparently had no effect on the men on the following days, for they pursued the retreating Ossorians and, despite courageous delaying tactics, finally routed them. In the ultimate three-day battle before the Ossory men's hastily constructed defences, near what is now Freshford, the Norse of Wexford led the attack and were repulsed many times. Then the Normans came up, stormed the entrenchments and routed MacGiolla Phadraig's men.

Dermot and his allies then went on into north Leinster and ravaged the territories of the O'Byrnes and O'Tooles as well as the lands of O'Connor of Offaly.

About this time there occurred an incident which proved a setback for MacMurrough. Maurice de Prendergast, 'a right valiunte captain' and apparently an honest and upright man, must have grown suspicious of Dermot's motives and chary of the success of the Norman adventurers while in alliance with him.[6]

Giraldus says: 'Dermot being grown proud with his victories gave discontentment to the English, insomuch that Maurice de Prendergast, with 200 soldiers, went to Wexford with the resolution to embark and pass into Wales.'

The author of *The Song of Dermot* writes:

> *This man departed from King Dermot*
> *Full two hundred he brought away with him*
> *Of the English in truth ...*
> *Towards Wexford he set out*
> *He wished to cross the sea to Wales*
> *Then the king sent word*
> *To Wexford by messenger*
> *All the master mariners*
> *He made obstruct Maurice*
> *So that he could not cross the sea.*

Maurice, however, was not to be baulked thus. He talked his way out of arrest by the Norse of Wexford, then sent word to MacGiolla Phadraig that he was willing to join him against Dermot.

'This he did,' says *The Song of Dermot*, 'and there the baron received the name of Maurice of Ossory.'

But de Prendergast's new-found allies soon grew jealous of him; they also disliked having to pay for his services. *The Song of Dermot* explains:

> *The men of Ossory*
> *Were much discontented*
> *That they had to hire soldiers*
> *And to give their pay to the English.*

Maurice, sensing their attitude and fearing an attempt to oust or kill him, asked MacGiolla Phadraig to allow him to return to Wales. The king of Ossory consented but his followers plotted to kill Maurice in an ambush as he and his men made their way to the coast. The plot was betrayed to Maurice, however, who pretended (to throw the men of Ossory off guard) that he was willing to stay in Ossory for another six months. He then took another route to Waterford where he and his 200 men took ship back to Wales.[7]

With the departure of de Prendergast, MacGiolla Phadraig decided that it was useless to continue the struggle and submitted – pointedly – to FitzStephen. The latter consulted with Dermot who insisted on MacGiolla Phadraig's acknowledging him as king of Leinster.

MacMurrough by this time, with the aid of his foreigners, had brought most of his former kingdom of Leinster back under his control.

We may wonder why High-King Ruairi O'Connor had not acted before this to stop Dermot and the invaders. History's judgment on Ruairi has not been flattering. He was a vacillating and timid man. 'His forte,' writes Charles B. Gibson, 'consisted in writing letters, making warlike speeches, and treating, *privately*, with his enemies.' But now the alarm of many of his subkings forced him to take some kind of action.

'An account of these events,' the chronicler in *Mac-Carthaig's Book* writes, 'reached Ruairi O'Connor who was titled king of Ireland at that time. He assembled those of the forces of Ireland who were his lieges, and went to Ferns.' This would have been sometime in the autumn.

Dermot and his allies withdrew into the dense forest of Dubh-tir, between Ferns and the mountains to the west, where they constructed defences and dug trenches among the trees and undergrowth.[8] Ruairi did not dare a mass assault on this position but sent in scouting parties 'to scour the forests and pursue the rebels'. The situation was saved by the intervention of the clergy: 'The bishops of the province, alarmed at the idea of a war breaking out among them, prostrated themselves at Ruairi's feet. Moved by the remonstrances of the bishops and clergy of Leinster, he ceased hostilities, and entered into negotia-

75 Ruairi O'Connor

tions with the king of the province.'[9]

Once again Dermot had been saved by his friends in the Church. The negotiations resulted in the Treaty of 1169 under which Dermot was allowed to retain the kingship of Leinster provided he recognised Ruairi as high-king of Ireland. Despite the fact that FitzStephen had earlier refused Ruairi's request that he leave the country, saying he could not let Dermot down, MacMurrough now, in a secret clause in the treaty, undertook to send his foreign allies back to Wales as soon as all Leinster was subdued: 'MacMurchadha was to send back the knights, and not to bring any more foreigners to Ireland, nor to support them there. He gave up his own halidoms and his son to O'Conchobhair in token of his fulfilment of that agreement.'[10]

The ancient chronicler of *MacCarthaigh's Book* is

obviously mistaken about another clause in the treaty. 'Diarmaid MacMurchadha was to receive O'Conchobhair's daughter as wife,' the translation reads; whereas what was undoubtedly agreed to was that Dermot's son Conor, who was handed over as hostage to Ruairi, would receive the latter's daughter in marriage in due course – if the treaty was adhered to.

The marriage never took place, for the treaty was soon broken. It is doubtful if MacMurrough ever had any intention of honouring it, for his sights were now fixed on the high-kingship itself, and he was probably playing for time. Besides, FitzStephen was indicating that he had no intention of returning to Wales.

A further landing of Normans, very soon afterwards, finally settled the question. This landing, the third, took place at Wexford, probably towards the end of 1169. *The Song of Dermot* tells us that Maurice FitzGerald landed with 'a goodly force and many followers, in order to aid King Dermot'. Giraldus says he brought with him in two ships 'ten men-at-arms, thirty mounted retainers and about a hundred archers and foot-soldiers'. (The *Annals of Inisfallen* put the number at 1,000 archers, but that would be far too many for only two ships.)

FitzGerald, half-brother of Robert FitzStephen, was undoubtedly intent on claiming his grant of Wexford town and the former Norse territory surrounding it. FitzStephen, incidentally, had started to lay out the defences on the borders of this cantred, by erecting a fortification on the cliff overlooking the Slaney at the place now called Ferrycarrig.[11]

Giraldus gives a flattering description of FitzGerald, who was his uncle:

A man of dignified aspect and modest bearing, of a ruddy complexion and good features. He was of the middle height, neither tall nor short. In him, both in person and temper moderation was the rule ...

Maurice was naturally of an excellent disposition, but he was much more anxious to *be* good than to appear such ... He was a man of few words, but his language was polished and there was more sense than sound, more reason than eloquence, in what he said ... In war he was intrepid, and second to no man in valour ... He was sober, modest, chaste, constant, firm and faithful; a man not altogether without fault, but not stained by any great and notorious crime.

He was, in his nephew's eyes, 'the pattern and model of his country and times'. At this time he would have been about sixty years of age, much older than the other invaders.

Dermot's welcome for the newcomer may well have been tempered by the knowledge that the die was now cast – the treaty with Ruairi was broken, and his own son's life was in danger.

Ruairi, in turn, must have been having a rapid change of opinion about 'the fleet of the Flemings' by which, as the *Annals of Tighernach* tell, he and his allies 'set nothing' (thought them not worth notice). The high-king marched his army out of Leinster but he must soon have known that Dermot had not sent his foreign allies back to Wales, and that, on the contrary, reinforcements had actually arrived under FitzGerald. Little did he realise that the invasion was, as yet, only getting under way, and that within a few months more and more invaders would be landing.

13
Baginbun

There is some confusion in the ancient chronicles as to whether Dermot, at this stage, marched on Dublin. Giraldus and the *Annals of Tighernach* agree that the march took place.

The arrival of Maurice FitzGerald with fresh troops may have swayed MacMurrough and, with the memory of his father's death and debasement at the hands of the Dublin Norsemen still rankling in his mind, he may have decided to avenge the deed.[1]

But, if he did march on the city, it apparently did not permit him the satisfaction of sacking it and punishing its citizens. The king of the Norse, Asculf MacTorkil or Asgall MacTorcaill, aware perhaps of the terms of the Treaty of 1169 (which gave Dermot jurisdiction over the Norse cities of Dublin and Waterford) submitted to him and gave him treasure and hostages.

About this time, also, Dermot felt strong enough to send a small body of Normans under FitzStephen all the way across the country to Limerick to aid his son-in-law Donal O'Brien, who was in conflict with High-King Ruairi. The success of this cross-country expedition must have proved to him, if proof were still needed, that his mail-clad allies, so far quite few in numbers compared with Ruairi's hosts, were almost invulnerable. If so few could achieve so much, what would a big army of Normans do? The answer to this question undoubtedly induced visions of the high-kingship itself.

Geoffrey Keating says that when Dermot saw how

76 *Raymond le Gros*

successfully his plans were maturing (Dublin having given treasure and hostages) he unfolded his plans for the takeover of all Ireland to FitzStephen and FitzGerald. They agreed that it would be easy if he had more men and that he should send to Wales for more. Dermot requested them to do the asking and, as a lure, promised to give his own daughter Aoife to whichever of them would accept her. But 'neither of them consented to accept her, for both remembered that MacMurchadha had promised that lady ... to the earl of Stranguell' (Strongbow).[2]

Then Dermot himself 'sent letters to England for Richard, earl of Striguil' (*MacCarthaigh's Book*). The letters urged Strongbow to redeem the promise made during their initial negotiations in 1167 and again dangled the lure of succession to the kingship of Leinster through marriage with Aoife.

This time Strongbow reacted. He had, no doubt, also received reports from his 'explorator', Hervey de Monte Marisco, and now realised that the prospects of the kingship of Leinster, and indeed of succession to the high-kingship, had vastly improved.

While he himself made his preparations he sent over an advance party under Raymond le Gros FitzGerald de Carew, nephew of Maurice FitzGerald and of Robert FitzStephen.

The Song of Dermot says:

> *Then soon afterwards*
> *Earl Richard sent over*
> *Some of his men to Ireland*
> *With nine or ten of his barons*
> *The first was Raymond le Gros,*
> *A bold and daring knight.*

Giraldus says Raymond brought with him ten men-at-arms and seventy archers. The date, once again, was around 1 May 1170. This was the fourth landing of the invasion.

The place where they landed was Baginbun, then known as Dundonnell. But, because of variations in the rendering of the name and in the location of the spot by the chroniclers of old, there has been a constant disputation among historians, down to the present day, about the landing-place.

Giraldus says Raymond and his small party landed at 'the rock of Dundunnolf', and adds that the spot was 'about four miles from Waterford, and to the south of Wexford'. According to Keating, Raymond 'put into port at Dun Domhnaill ... four miles south of Port Lairge'. Hooker calls the place 'Dundonough' and says it was a rock in the county of Waterford, eight miles east of the city and twelve miles south of Wexford.[3] *The Song of Dermot* merely gives the place-name: 'At Dundonuil they landed.'

Down the intervening centuries, several other places have been mentioned as the landing-place of Raymond: Dundrone, four miles from Waterford; Don-isle, in Waterford, a place now called 'Dunhill' (Charles Smith in *History of Waterford*); and 'Drumdowney, about five or six miles north from Waterford, by a ford over the Barrow and beetling over the junction of the three rivers, the united Nore and Barrow and Suir.' (Rev James Graves).

The persistent tradition is that Baginbun (Dundonnell) was the actual landing-place of Raymond, and to my mind irrefutable evidence in support of this has been put forward by Orpen.[4]

He draws his data from (1) Giraldus: *Applicantes itaque in rupe quadam marina, quae Dundunnolf dicitur, a Waterfordiae miliaribus quasi quatuor, a latere Weisefordiae meridionali, tenue satis ex vergis et cespite castrum erexerunt.* ('Landing at the rock of Dundunnolf, which lies on the sea coast, about four miles from Waterford, and to the south of Wexford, they threw up a rather slight fortification, made of turf and boughs of trees.'); (2) *The Song of Dermot,* where the name of the place is variously rendered as

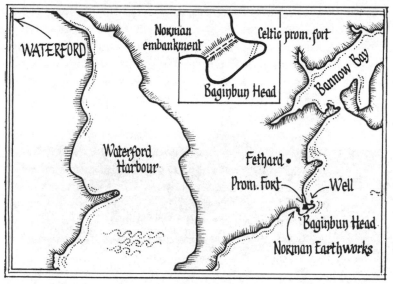

77 Map of Baginbun area

Domdonuil, Dondonuil and Dundounil – from which it may be concluded, says Orpen, that the Irish name of the place was Dun Domhnaill (Dundonnell).

In explanation of the statement by Giraldus that Dundunnolf was 'about four miles' from Waterford, Orpen says:

> The Roman mile was equal to 1,618 English yards, and Baginbun is about thirteen English miles (as an arrow flies) from Waterford. The following considerations, however, will go far to remove the force of this objection. Nothing is more easily corrupted in the course of transcribing Latin manuscripts than Roman numerals. Leave out the X and XIV becomes IV. In the present case it is certain either that some corruption of the kind had occurred or that Gerald was very inaccurate in his statement (for no place within a radius of four miles from Waterford could be described as on the southern side of Wexford). In fact Baginbun is about the nearest place to Waterford that could be so

78 Baginbun

described with any approach to accuracy. We have proof of Gerald's inaccuracy as regards distances in other places. He says the town of Wexford was distant from Bannow *milia passuum quasi duodecim*, whereas it is upwards of sixteen statute miles as the crow flies.

Orpen finds further hints in Giraldus as to the true location of the landing-place, notably his statement that the citizens of Waterford and O'Faolain of the Decies crossed the Suir to attack Raymond's entrenchments. This would place them at Baginbun. The estuary into which the rivers Barrow, Nore and Suir flow is still called the Suir by the Waterford people.

Giraldus, continues Orpen, says that numbers of the vanquished were hurled *'ab altis in mare rupibus'*, 'On these data,' says Orpen, 'the Rev Mr. Graves is said to have identified the place with a precipitous rock now called Drumdowny.'

Orpen points out the inconsistencies in this contention: Drumdowny is *not* 'four or five miles north from Waterford'; it is four miles north-east. It is *not* by a ford; it is by a ferry. It is *not* beetling over the junction of the three rivers; it is, in fact, one mile above the junction. Strengthening his case further, Orpen says Drum Domhnaigh is quite distinct from Dun Domhnaill. While the three rivers are tidal, it is stretching the imagination, he suggests, to say that Drumdowny is a *rupes marina* (a sea cliff). Besides, Drumdowney is not *a latere Weisefordiae meridionali* (on the south side of Wexford); it is not in Dermot's territory, but in Ossory, the territory of Dermot's enemies and therefore a most unlikely place for Raymond to select for his encampment.

The Song of Dermot says that Raymond and his men 'constructed a fort, by the permission of the rich king, Dermot'. Thus it must have been in Dermot's territory.

Orpen feels that Baginbun has so much in its favour that it must be accepted as Raymond's landing-place.

There is tradition – never to be ignored. There is the Irish name which implies a Celtic dún and, indeed, Orpen and others think that some of the entrenchments still to be seen at Baginbun Head may be Celtic in origin.[5]

We have the statements of our contemporary chroniclers and of Keating that Raymond constructed defences of some kind on Baginbun Head. Giraldus says he 'threw up a rather slight fortification, made of turf and boughs of trees'.[6] Keating describes the defences as a 'strong embankment of stones and clay'.[7] If, as I maintain, the entrenchments across the narrow neck of the main head at Baginbun are Norman in origin, then Keating's description fits best. There is a double embankment with a deep trench between, forty feet wide at the top, running the entire width of the 200 yards wide headland. It is, as Keating says, built of stones and clay and, except for an overgrowth of furze and some despoliation as a result of gaps being broken in a few places, the entrenchment is much the same today as it was in 1170. It runs straight across the headland, abutting on the high cliffs on either side, with a gentle, open slope leading up to the outer embankment, and it must have presented a formidable obstacle to any attackers, particularly when confronted with Raymond's archers and their ever-shifting field of fire.

There is quite a difference between this outer entrenchment and the ancient earthworks across the neck of the smaller promontory to the east, called Baginbun Point. The passage of time has worn the sides of these works into uneven slopes, unlike the outer embankments which are still steep-sided. Further, the inner works are slightly elliptical while the outer ones are straight.

While Rev James Graves dismisses the story of the Normans entrenching themselves at Baginbun as 'a mere myth without slightest foundation', he has 'no doubt' that the 'elaborate fosses and ramparts should be referred to the primaeval inhabitants of the country'. For such an

79 *Giving the order*

assertion he has little authority. On the contrary, there is much written evidence that the outer defence-works, at least, are of Norman origin.

Orpen has no doubts. In a detailed description of Baginbun and its earthworks he refers to the well-preserved fosse and rampart across the neck of the headland, then mentions the further rocky headland cut off from the other by 'a probably still more ancient ditch'.[8] On this smaller point, he says, are the remains of 'other earthworks'.[9]

All such considerations apart, there is every reason to believe that Baginbun was quite deliberately chosen by Raymond as an ideal landing-place. It was in Dermot's territory, as we have seen. It was just across the bay from Bannow and was probably surveyed by the earlier invaders. It was in an advantageous position from which to command a sea entry to Waterford Harbour. It was easily defended, once defences had been thrown up on the landward side. It had a small, but suitable, beach where ships could be drawn up, and a sheltered cove where they could, alternatively, be anchored. It had a freshwater supply; there is a never-failing spring in the Mine Holes,

80 ... to build fortifications

near the beach on the northern side of Baginbun Point.

So, at Baginbun then, about 1 May 1170, Raymond and his small army landed and set about preparing the place for defence.[10] He knew Strongbow was to follow but did not know exactly when. In the meantime he had to secure his bridgehead.

He was joined shortly, according to Giraldus, by Hervey de Monte Marisco with three knights (and perhaps a small body of men) but, all told, the little army at Baginbun still numbered no more than a hundred. He threw up the temporary defences in haste, rounded up as many cattle in the area as he could and drove them within the stockade.

> *There Raymond le Gros remained*
> *With his knights and barons*
> *Then he plundered the territory*
> *Took and killed the cows.*[11]

These cattle, collected initially to provide meat (and milk?), were to play a rather different part in Raymond's plans before long. At this stage he may have commenced the construction of the more durable earthworks across

81 The final charge

the neck of the headland but, with fewer than a hundred men, can hardly have made much progress in this colossal task when the first attack on his position was mounted.

The Song of Dermot says:

> But the men of Waterford
> And of Ossory likewise
> Assembled their hosts,
> Against Dundonuil they resolved to go
> In order to attack the fort.

The annalist in *MacCarthaigh's Book* says that the army of the Irish and the Waterford Norsemen numbered 3,000. With this number Giraldus agrees, adding that Raymond and his followers 'inferior as they were in numbers, with surpassing gallantry, sallied forth and engaged in the too unequal conflict'.

The place where Raymond and his men met the advance guard of the Norse-Irish army may have been Battlestown (was it named after the encounter?), about two miles beyond Fethard in the direction of Ballyhack. Seeing that they were outnumbered Raymond ordered his followers back to the defences of Baginbun.

82 ... as the defenders flee

According to Giraldus:

> Their small band of soldiers was, however, unable to resist the attack of the multitudes to which they were opposed; and retreating to their camp, they were so hotly pursued by the enemy that some of them entered pell-mell with the fugitives before the barricade could be closed.

In this critical situation, Raymond showed his qualities as a leader and a soldier. Giraldus again:

> Raymond perceiving the strait to which his party was reduced and, in short, that the peril was imminent, faced about boldly and cut down with his sword, on the very threshold, the foremost of the enemy who were forcing an entrance.[12]

MacCarthaigh's Book takes up the story:

> ... when the crowd nearest (of Norse and Irish) saw this, they at once fled towards their people, and when the rearguard saw the van fleeing towards them, they too fled, and the English pursued them and inflicted

slaughter on them by drowning and by killing.'

Giraldus gives a livelier and more colourful description of Raymond's part in routing the attackers:

> Thus nobly retracing his steps, while he dealt a terrible blow and shouted his war-cry, he encouraged his followers to stand on their defence, and struck terror into the enemies' ranks ... the enemy took to flight and, dispersing themselves over the country, were pursued and slaughtered in such numbers that upwards of 500 quickly fell by the sword; and when the pursuers ceased striking from sheer weariness, they threw vast numbers from the edge of the cliffs into the sea underneath.

Giraldus makes no mention, however, of a *ruse de guerre* adopted by Raymond and described by the author of *The Song of Dermot*. He says Raymond addressed his men, then drove the herd of cows which he had rounded up out among the attackers causing confusion and disarray.[13] Following up the advantage:

> *Raymond with his English*
> *Threw himself amid the Irish.*

with the result that 1,000 Irish were killed, wounded or taken prisoner. Giraldus, intent on extolling the bravery of his kinsman, ascribes the victory at Baginbun to the prowess of Raymond and another Norman named William Ferrand: 'In this engagement a certain man-at-arms, whose name was William Ferrand, exhibited undaunted courage. His body was weak, but his spirit resolute; for being diseased with leprosy, which threatened his life, he sought to anticipate the effects of a disease by a premature though glorious death.'

William Ferrand did not succeed in meeting a glorious death that day, and lived to achieve a slight fame of another sort. He later founded the Leper Church of St

Magdalen outside Wexford town (the district is now known as Maudlintown, a corruption of Magdalen's town) and is probably buried in the leper cemetery which was then attached to the church and the leper hospital beside it.

Having routed the Norse-Irish army, the Normans were undecided about what to do with the seventy prisoners they had taken. They were men of some importance in Waterford and the initial idea may have been to ransom them.

Giraldus describes what followed: 'The English abused their good fortune by evil and detestable counsels and inhuman cruelty; for having gained the victory, they kept seventy of the principal townsmen prisoners in the camp, for whose ransom they might have obtained the city itself or an immense sum of money.'

Hervey and Raymond argued about what should be done with the prisoners, Hervey, according to Giraldus (who obviously preferred his kinsman Raymond to de Monte Marisco), saying that mercy was out of place and that the prisoners outnumbered the guards, thus constituting a threat in themselves; Raymond pleading that they should be merely held to ransom: 'Hervey's opinion was approved by his comrades, and the wretched captives, as men condemned, had their limbs broken and were cast headlong into the sea and drowned.'

The narrator of *The Song of Dermot* adds a grisly climax to this inhuman deed. He says:

> *Of the Irish there were taken*
> *Quite as many as seventy*
> *But the noble knights*
> *Had them beheaded.*
> *To a wench they gave*
> *An axe of tempered steel*
> *And she beheaded them all*
> *And then threw their bodies over the cliff*

83 Hervey de Monte Marisco

Because she had that day
Lost her lover in the combat.
Alice of Abervenny was her name
Who served the Irish thus.

This Alice may have been a camp-follower who accompanied her lover from Wales. If the story of the multiple beheading be true, she must have been an Amazon, or so berserk in her sorrow and rage at losing her man that she found a strength fierce enough to enable her to wield the death-axe so often.

Raymond himself, described by Giraldus as 'prudent and temperate, liberal, kind and circumspect', would hardly have countenanced such brutality but on this occasion he was apparently overruled by the more callous Hervey – Strongbow's special envoy and a man, therefore, of some authority.

Giraldus did not like Hervey, whom he described as 'a spy rather than a soldier', probably because, as Strongbow's right-hand man and 'explorator' (investigator), he was in a position to command Giraldus's own relatives, Raymond, FitzGerald and FitzStephen. Thus Giraldus makes him responsible for the decision to execute the prisoners and indirectly so for the manner of their deaths. For these decisions Hervey, according to Giraldus, 'was loaded with weighty and lasting disgrace and infamy; nor could one be found whom his carnage of the citizens did not disgust'.

Whether or not Hervey was wholly responsible, we may rightly infer that the deed was more in keeping with his dark and designing nature than with young Raymond of whom Giraldus gives this graphic description:

... very stout and a little above the middle height; his hair was yellow and curly and he had large, grey, round eyes. His nose was rather prominent, his countenance high-coloured, cheerful and pleasant; and although he was somewhat corpulent, he was so lively and active

that the incumbrance was not a blemish or inconvenience. Such was his care of his troops that he passed
whole nights without sleep, going the rounds of the
guards himself, and challenging the sentinels to keep
them on the alert ... Thinking more how he could
promote the welfare of his men, than of commanding
them, he was their servant rather than their master ...
Although a daring soldier and consummate general,
even in military affairs prudence was his highest
quality.

Altogether, we may sum up, a jolly, likeable fellow and a
good man to have at one's side at wine or in war.[14]

Strongbow's choice of the man to lead his advance
party and secure his bridgehead was a good one. His
prudence now paid off. Another man might have
followed up the rout of the Norse and Irish by an attempt
on Waterford itself. But Raymond remained, wisely, behind his fortifications at Baginbun. He stayed there, in
fact, all summer until Strongbow himself arrived on 23
August. Raymond must have known that Dermot, having
been weakened by the defection of Maurice de Prendergast to Ossory, was in no position to help him. Similarly
Robert FitzStephen was otherwise engaged, having gone
on his cross-country expedition to aid Donal O'Brien at
Limerick.

Thus Raymond, secure within his entrenchments, preferred to await the reinforcements he knew were coming
under Strongbow before undertaking any further military
operations.

It has been stated that Raymond's victory at Baginbun
can justly be singled out as a real turning-point, not only
in the invasion but also in Irish history. Had Raymond's
little army been wiped out, Strongbow himself, even with
his much stronger forces, would probably have been
intimidated from a further major landing. FitzStephen's
power would have withered without such reinforcement

and, in time, he would have been defeated and driven out of Ireland by the superior numbers of the high-king and his allies. Without the expansion of Norman power into the country the history of Ireland would have been very different.

Small wonder, then, that Stanihurst noted that:[15]

> *At the creeke of Baginbunne*
> *Ireland was lost and wonne.*

84 *Tomb effigy of Raymond le Gros*

14
Strongbow

Giraldus describes the embarkation and landing of the biggest of the Norman task-forces to date:

> Meanwhile Earl Richard, having prepared all things necessary for so great an enterprise, took his journey to St David's along the coast of south Wales, adding to his numbers picked youths from the districts through which he passed. When all was ready for the important voyage, he betook himself to the port of Milford, and embarking there with about 200 men-at-arms, and other troops, to the number of 1,000 sailed over to Waterford with a fair wind and landed there on the tenth of the calends of September, being the eve of the feast of St Bartholomew.

Strongbow had taken the precaution of seeking Henry's approval for the expedition – which approval, we are told, the king gave in jest, 'urging him on as far as his feet could bear him'.

85 Making ships for invasion

Well may Henry have been derisive, for he was thus ridding himself of one of his most troublesome subjects.

Strongbow landed at Passage on 23 August 1170. As his fleet passed along the south coast of Wexford and before it rounded Rinn a' Dubhain (Hook Head) to enter Waterford estuary, it had undoubtedly been seen by Raymond and his men entrenched at Baginbun. What a mighty cheer must have gone up as the Norman ships passed along the horizon! We can safely assume that Raymond had been kept informed of preparations for the expedition and that a courier was now sent to Baginbun in a smaller vessel to tell him of Strongbow's plans and to co-ordinate the movements of the two armies.

Then, for the first time in three months, Raymond led his men out of their stronghold and marched northwards a few miles to Duncannon or Ballyhack where there were ferries plying across the estuary. He must have crossed the tidal waters without difficulty for Giraldus tells us that on the following morning (24 August) his banners were already displayed against the walls of Waterford by the time Strongbow brought up his force. The combined armies then advanced to make the assault on the town.

Waterford at the time was a Norse stronghold but among the defenders were numerous Irish from the Decies under their chief, Maolseachlann O Faolain (O'Phelan), who had taken part in the May attack on Raymond's fortified position at Baginbun. The town was

86 ... and pulling them to the sea

87 Reginald's Tower

defended by ramparts of stone and clay with, at strategic points, round stone towers.

Two attacks by the Normans on these walls were repulsed. Then Raymond (the valiant soldier whom Giraldus never leaves out of the picture for long) 'discovering a little house of timber standing upon a post, outside the wall, to which it also hung, loudly called on the assailants from all quarters to renew the assault, and sent men in armour to hew down the post'. In modern military parlance, Raymond called for 'covering fire' while an assault party attacked this weak spot in the defences.

Giraldus continues: 'As soon as it was done, the house fell, and carried with it a great piece of the wall, and the assailants, entering manfully through the breach, rushed into the town and, slaughtering the citizens in heaps along the streets, gained a very bloody victory.'

The towers on the walls were the last posts to fall. One of them, Reginald's Tower, was fiercely defended by a small group of Norse and Irish which included two Norse earls named Sitric, another Norse leader named Reginald (after whom the tower was named) and O Faolain of the Decies.

The two Sitrics were executed after being taken prisoner. Reginald and O Faolain owed their lives to Dermot MacMurrough who arrived after the fall of the town and pleaded for them. The date was 25 August.

With Dermot had arrived Robert FitzStephen, Maurice FitzGerald, and his daughter Aoife. And there, in the smoking, reeking town, with the dead lying in piles in the streets and the wounded moaning in the lanes and byways, Dermot gave his daughter in marriage to Earl Richard in fulfilment of his promise.

We can picture the scene in the church in Waterford on that fateful day in August 1170, with the mail-clad Normans and their Flemish, Welsh and Irish allies cramming the aisles to catch a glimpse of the famed Strongbow and his bride.[1] Giraldus tells us that Aoife was possessed of 'exceeding beauty'. As for the earl, the Welsh historian has left us this portrait:

> His complexion was somewhat ruddy, and his skin freckled; he had grey eyes, feminine features, a weak voice, and short neck. For the rest he was tall in stature, and a man of great generosity and of courteous manner. What he failed of accomplishing by force, he succeeded in by gentle words. In time of peace he was more disposed to be led by others than to command. Out of the camp he had more the air of an ordinary man-at-arms than of a general-in-chief; but in action the mere soldier was forgotten in the commander. With the advice of those about him he was ready to dare anything, but he never ordered any attack relying on his own judgment, or rashly presuming on his personal

courage. The post he occupied in battle was a sure rallying point for his troops. His equanimity and firmness in all the vicissitudes of war were remarkable, being neither driven to despair in adversity nor puffed up by success.

Such was the man who, by this first Norman-Irish marriage after the invasion, became heir-in-succession to the kingdom of Leinster and the Norse towns of Dublin, Waterford and Wexford, whenever Dermot should die. MacMurrough was, of course, breaking Irish law in delivering his kingdom thus to a son-in-law, particularly an outsider. He was contravening the long-accepted practice whereby his sons and his brother had the right to be chosen as king by the entire tribe. But Dermot's ambition and burning vengefulness overrode all such considerations. He needed the Normans to regain and retain his kingdom and to avenge his earlier defeats, particularly that suffered at the hands of his mortal enemy O'Rourke. He was, no doubt, also remembering his father's death at the hands of the Norse of Dublin. The stage had now been reached, however, when it was Strongbow and the invaders who set the terms; Dermot became the mere instrument by which their attempt at conquest was initiated – from now on (for the short remaining span of his life) he was in the power of the very forces he himself had brought to Ireland and unleashed.

Success in the field was still all-important for both Dermot and the invaders. Dublin seemed the obvious next target. Though only a small, well-fortified trading-centre, its possession carried with it considerable political and religious advantages. Besides being a meeting-place for foreign merchants and traders, it was the residence of an archbishop, occasionally of the king of Leinster, and a strategic post for the command of the eastern entrance to the rich hinterlands of Meath and Kildare.

88 Strongbow

High-King Ruairi O'Connor also realised the strategic and political value of Dublin. Although beset by the O'Briens, who had rebelled against him, he mustered a huge army and marched to guard the southern and western approaches to the city. With O'Connor, as usual, was Tiernan O'Rourke.

The Norman-Irish forces had meanwhile been marching through Wexford and into Wicklow. Giraldus details the composition of the army as it advanced:

> Milo de Cogan, a gentleman of great worth and valour, marched in the van, with a regiment 700 strong, accompanied by Donal Cavanagh, Dermot's son, and his Irish troops. Next Raymond le Gros, of whose praise and worthiness enough cannot be said, led the battle with his regiment of 800 English, and with him the king of Leinster, with a thousand of his followers. The rear, with 3,000 English, was commanded by the earl (Strongbow), and in the rear of him a regiment of Irish.

Giraldus's figures cannot be relied on here. The total numbers of invaders who had landed to date could not have exceeded 2,000. Where the extra 2,000 men came from we do not know – unless reinforcements followed Strongbow to Waterford which went unrecorded. It is more likely that the balance of 3,500 of the Norman-Irish army was made up of Irish and Norse.

Against this 5,500 main force, the high-king, according to Giraldus, had mustered 30,000 troops. This figure also must be doubted and reduced by at least a half. Ruairi's men were numerous enough, however, to hold all the passes west and south-west of Dublin. The main force camped at Clondalkin. 'The pride of Ireland were gathered at Clondalkin on the moor,' says *The Song of Dermot*.

MacMurrough, however, succeeded in eluding the high-king's patrols by leading the Norman-Irish army through little-known passes over the Wicklow mountains, past Glendalough, and down the forested foothills to where Rathfarnham now is. His knowledge of the terrain served him and his allies well, for they arrived before the southern walls of Dublin unhindered and proceeded to invest the city.

The Norman-Irish troops thus drove a wedge between Ruairi's army and Dublin. The Norse within the city, after some feeble attempts to break the ring of steel round their stronghold, offered to negotiate. They sent Archbishop Laurence O'Toole (Dermot's brother-in-law) to sue for peace. The emissary of Dermot and Strongbow on this occasion was Morice Regan, MacMurrough's secretary. During the negotiations a truce was agreed on.

The Song of Dermot infers that during the peace parleys Raymond le Gros and Milo de Cogan approached the walls from different directions and, acting without orders from Dermot or Strongbow, burst into the city. According to Giraldus: 'Raymond on one side of the city and Milo de Cogan on the other rushed to the walls with bands of youths, and making a resolute assault, got possession of the place with great slaughter of the citizens.'

Asculf MacTorkil, the king of Dublin, together with the chief men of the city, barely had time to reach their ships in the harbour, whence they sailed away to their kinsfolk in the Orkney Islands, vowing to return one day to avenge their defeat.

MacCarthaigh's Book records the fall of Dublin, on 21 September 1170:

> MacMurchadha and the earl went with their knights to Dublin and they drove out all the Norse, the merchants and the inhabitants who were there, killed or drowned many women and men and youths, and carried off much gold and silver and apparel. The English earl left the care of these, as well as of the town, in the hands of Diarmaid MacMurchadha to avenge the

89 Wall painting, Moy Cathedral

wicked slaying of his father by the people of Dublin before that, when a dead dog was buried with his body in the ground as a mark of hatred and contempt.

Even after fifty-five years Dermot's revenge must still have tasted sweet. There was still O'Rourke to be dealt with, however. But where was he and, for that matter, where was Ruairi with his great army?

It appears that when the Norse of Dublin commenced negotiations with Dermot and Strongbow, Ruairi and O'Rourke felt indignant and betrayed and marched away.

Dermot followed up his advantage by pursuing O'Rourke. The annalists record his depredations: 'An army was led by MacMurchadha, with his knights, into Meath and Breffni, and they plundered Clonard, Kells, Tailltin, Dowth, Slane, Dulane, Kilskeery and Castle Kieran, and they afterwards made a predatory incursion into Tir Briuin, and carried off many persons and cows to their camp'.2

But Dermot, although he failed to catch up with the elusive O'Rourke, had now gone too far. In invading Meath and Breifne he had broken the Treaty of 1169 and he was sharply reminded of this by Ruairi, who had kept his army mobilised and was watching Dermot's moves. Under the terms of the 1169 treaty Dermot was confined to his own kingdom of Leinster – in effect forbidden to invade other men's territories.

Ruairi's envoys, carrying the high-king's messages of protest and warning, were treated contemptuously by Dermot, who in turn remitted to O'Connor his own plans. He intended, he announced, to defeat the high-king's army and to claim the high-kingship for himself.

In the face of this threat Ruairi had to take some sort of action. What he did, however, was barbaric.

The *Four Masters* record: 'The hostages of Diarmaid were put to death by Ruairi O'Connor at Athlone, namely Conor, the son of Diarmaid, the heir-apparent of Leinster, and his grandson, that is the son of Donal Cavanagh, and the son of his foster-brother, that is O'Kelly.'

Ruairi may have hoped to deter Dermot by this drastic step. Or, in a rage at MacMurrough's blatant perfidy, he may have ordered the executions in a rash moment. The Irish annalists have made no attempt to justify the deed, thereby exposing its brutality. Further, according to Leland, the annalists 'speak in such terms of this hostage (Conor) – the noblest and most amiable youth in Leinster – as plainly show their detestation of this brutal cruelty of Roderick'.[3]

After this Dermot retired to Ferns and we hear little more of him. He may have been in failing health and undoubtedly the death of Conor would have affected him. About the beginning of May 1171 he died. According to the *Book of Leinster* he was sixty-one years of age.[4] His death is recorded in the *Annals of the Four Masters*:

> Dermot MacMurrough, king of Leinster, who had spread terror throughout Ireland, after putting the English in possession of the country, committing excessive evils against the Irish people, and plundering and burning many churches, among which were Kells, Clonard, and others, died this year of an intolerable and uncommon disease. He became putrid while living, by the miracles of God, through the intercession of Columcille, Finian and other saints of Ireland, for having violated and burned their churches. He died at Ferns without making a will, without penance, without the Eucharist, and without Extreme Unction, as his evil deeds deserved.

The scribes of the annals may have liked to believe that Dermot died thus, without benefit of the sacraments. But there is also evidence to the contrary. The *Book of Leinster* says he died 'after the victory of unction and penance'; the author of *The Song of Dermot* merely that he 'died at Ferns'. Since his good friends and beneficiaries, the Augustinian monks of St Mary's at Ferns, were so close at hand, it is unlikely that they would have allowed him to die without the last sacraments, particularly when his demise was a lingering one.[5]

Dermot is reputedly buried in Ferns churchyard where the broken shaft of a cross, ornamented with a Celtic

design, is said to mark his grave. In the adjoining field
there stand the striking ruins of the Augustinian abbey
where he once found refuge, while not far away are the
shattered remains of Ferns Castle, a Norman structure
which probably occupies the site of Dermot's own 'stone
house'.

Sic transit . . . .

90 Ferns Castle

15

Siege

After the fall of Dublin, Milo de Cogan was appointed its military governor, while Strongbow returned to the south to consolidate his Leinster bridgehead. There were now Norman garrisons in Waterford, Dublin and Wexford and the Irish kings and hierarchy began to be alarmed at the situation.

The concern of the Church manifested itself in the convening of a general synod in Armagh towards the end of 1170, when the invasion was declared to be a judgment for the sins of the people 'and especially for that they had long been wont to purchase natives of England from traders, robbers and pirates, and to reduce them to slavery'.[1] The synod decreed that all Englishmen throughout Ireland who were slaves should be set free. Whether the Church hoped to assuage Norman ire by this action cannot be ascertained. Perhaps, with that uncanny instinct for backing the right horse, the ecclesiastical authorities hoped to win the approval of the future rulers of the country.

The Irish kings and chieftains, even after the fall of Waterford and Dublin, still seemed unaware of the peril presented to their positions by the invaders. As far as most of them were concerned, this was a private fight between Dermot MacMurrough and the high-king, with a few foreigners aiding Dermot.

But MacMurrough's death, in May 1171, and Strongbow's accession to the kingship of Leinster, changed all that. If a foreigner could climb on to the throne of Leinster so quickly and so easily, then it was time to defend their own interests. Not only was their law of succession being cast aside but Strongbow, by his appointment of officials in the occupied territories and towns, was also setting up a new system of government and law which was alien to the Irish.

The tribes of Leinster, even those who had been

91 A deed issued by Strongbow

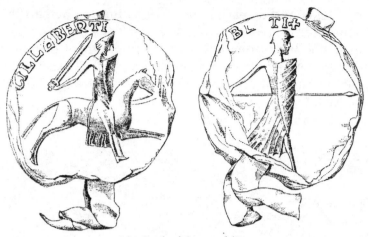

92 *Seal of Strongbow*

supporters of Dermot, rose in revolt against Strongbow. Dermot's son, Donal Cavanagh, remained on the earl's side, but Dermot's nephew, Murchadh, led the revolting clans of Uí Ceinnsealaigh against the invaders.

High-King Ruairi called on the provincial kings of Ireland to rally immediately to drive out the foreigner and many of them answered his call. And back from the northern islands sailed Asculf MacTorkil, with Norsemen in a fleet of sixty ships, determined to recapture Dublin and avenge their recent defeat.

The position for Strongbow and his barons looked serious, and no one realised it more profoundly than he. Faced with, for once, a united Irish army vastly superior in numbers to his own and allied forces, he could not hope for any help or reinforcements from Wales or England. Even before Dermot's death, Henry II, having heard with concern of Strongbow's successes in Ireland, had sent messages forbidding any more of his subjects to go to Ireland and ordering those already there to return home before Easter. Henry also banned the shipment of exports (and consequently, supplies for Strongbow) to Ireland. To cap all this Robert FitzStephen was being besieged in his fort at Ferrycarrig by the Wexford Norse who had also risen in revolt.

Earl Richard, according to Giraldus, sent Raymond le Gros with a letter to Henry (who was in Aquitaine) offering all his Irish possessions to the king. In the letter Strongbow pointed out that it was with Henry's permission that he had gone to aid Dermot 'your liegeman', and added, 'Whatever lands I have the good fortune to acquire here, either from his patrimony or that of any other, as I owe them to your grace I shall hold them at your will and disposal.'

Whether Strongbow hoped that this assurance would persuade Henry to allow more men and supplies into Ireland for further conquests, or whether he hoped Henry would permit him a free hand in Ireland, we cannot say. It may be that Richard was genuine in his offer and thus was renouncing any intention of setting up a rival Norman state in Ireland. In this he was alone, for his barons such as FitzStephen and FitzGerald were still as ambitious as ever to carve out a new kingdom in Ireland, with themselves as rulers.

Henry, who did not reply to Strongbow's letter, must have pondered deeply on its contents. Sooner or later he would have to act in regard to Strongbow, his barons and Ireland. As astute as ever, he decided to wait for the outcome of the critical situation in which Earl Richard now found himself. But his caution (and jealousy of Strongbow perhaps) nearly lost him any chance he had of winning Ireland.

If an overall plan existed for the extermination of the invaders it must have entailed a great national effort under Ruairi O'Connor to drive out the Normans, together with simultaneous uprisings in Leinster and in the former Norse strongholds of Waterford and Wexford, and the advent of a Norse fleet to cut Dublin off by sea.

The first part of the Irish-Norse campaign was marked

with successes. Waterford was recaptured by Dermot MacCarthy of Desmond. The Norsemen of Wexford drove FitzStephen into his fort at Ferrycarrig and laid siege to him there, and the Norse fleet under MacTorkil arrived in the Liffey. But from then on things went wrong.

MacTorkil's fleet disembarked the thousand Norse warriors under John the Wode (or Mad) and immediately, without waiting for Ruairi's great army to arrive and besiege the city, they launched an attack on the east gate.

Giraldus describes these Norsemen as born warriors, armed in the Danish fashion, some in long coats of mail, others with breastplates fastened to their tunics. All carried round shields painted red and rimmed with iron. They were 'men with iron hearts as well as iron arms'. Wielding their favourite weapon, the broad battle-axe, these massed Norsemen might even have been the match of the Norman infantry. They could not, however, withstand a Norman cavalry charge.

Milo de Cogan, Giraldus tells us, led an initial sally against the advancing Norsemen but, because of inferior numbers, he had to fall back inside the gate after losing some of his men, 'one of whom had his leg cut off by a single stroke of a battle-axe, though it was cased in iron armour on both sides'.

Richard de Cogan, Milo's brother, meanwhile got out unobserved at the head of a small body of troops and attacked the Norsemen from the rear. This may have been the cavalry attack referred to in other accounts of the engagement. Led by Richard de Cogan, the mounted knights charged the Norsemen, who finally broke and scattered. As they fled back to their ships they were cut down by the mounted Normans. The berserk John was killed, Asculf was captured and later beheaded after a trial in the hall of his own former palace in the city.[2]

For the moment Dublin was saved. But Ruairi's army had begun to march and was nearing the city. Besides O'Connor himself with his Connachtmen, the hosting included Tiernan O'Rourke (Breifne), Murchadh O'Carroll (Oriel), Murchadh MacMurrough (Leinster), Donal O'Brien (Thomond) and several other subkings with their levies.

The main body of this 60,000 strong army camped in the Castleknock area, while the Munster and Leinster men took up positions at Kilmainham and Dalkey and the Ulster men spread themselves in the Clontarf area.[3] In Dublin Bay there arrived a fleet of thirty ships carrying Norsemen from the Isle of Man and the Hebrides, commanded by Gottred, the king of Man. A request for aid had been sent to him at the behest of Archbishop Laurence O'Toole, who had supported High-King Ruairi in the mobilisation of the forces now encircling Dublin.

Within the beleaguered city, Strongbow, who had re-turned from Ferns after visiting the dying Dermot, assumed command. As the siege progressed from July into August the situation became desperate. Food grew steadily scarcer until, at length, supplies for only about a fortnight remained.[4] Strongbow decided to negotiate and sent for Archbishop O'Toole to whom he delivered his terms for surrender. The earl offered to submit to Ruairi

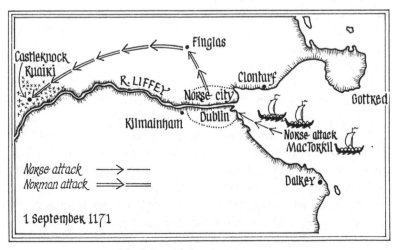

93 Map of the Dublin area

and to hold Leinster under the high-king if he would lift the siege.

O'Connor, confident that the Normans were on the point of defeat, laid down stringent conditions. He would leave Strongbow in control of the three Norse centres only – Dublin, Waterford and Wexford; if the earl spurned this offer he (O'Connor) would storm Dublin immediately.

Strongbow's council of war debated the terms. The earl himself may have wavered but not so his daring barons, particularly Milo de Cogan, Maurice FitzGerald and Raymond le Gros. Milo advocated a last desperate sortie.[5] Maurice also advised instant action, asking:

> Is it succour from our country that we expect? Nay, such is our lot that what the Irish are to the English we, too, being now considered Irish, are the same. The one island does not hold us in greater desperation than the other. Away, then, with hesitation and cowardice, and let us boldly attack the enemy, while our short stock of provisions yet supplies us with sufficient strength.[6]

Raymond concurred and said that they should attack O'Connor first as, with him defeated, they would have little difficulty dealing with the rest. The plans for the sortie were laid. Three detachments, each of 200 men and led by Strongbow, Milo and Raymond, were formed. No Irish were included as their 'fidelity and valour', according to *The Song of Dermot*, were not trusted. Donal Cavanagh, however, and one or two others are honourably exempted in this account and Donal, in fact, accompanied Raymond's contingent out of the city.

With Milo in the van, Raymond next and Strongbow bringing up the rear, the Normans crossed the Liffey, made a detour by Finglas and burst upon Ruairi's Liffey-side encampment at Castleknock.

On that sultry day in late summer the besiegers were in relaxed mood. The high-king and many of his men were bathing in the river when the attack came. The surprise was total. About 150 of the Irish were killed and the rest routed. Ruairi himself barely escaped with his life.

Hanmer says: 'Roderick took his ease and pleasure, and was bathing himself; but when the alarm was up, and he saw his men, on every side, fall to the ground, he never tarried or called for man or page to array him, but took his mantle and ran away, all naked.'[7]

The siege was lifted and O'Connor's army dispersed. The other contingents, which had guarded the southern and northern exits from the city, had either left already on raiding missions or now departed without striking a blow on hearing of Ruairi's defeat. The Irish camp was plundered and found to contain much welcome corn, meal and pork, sufficient 'for a whole year'.

The Normans had once more demonstrated their supremacy in arms.[8]

The date, according to Giraldus, was about 1 September 1171, a significant date in the chronicle of the invasion. It marks a radical change in the fortunes of the invaders and the beginning of the end for Ruairi O'Connor, the last high-king of Ireland. Following this, his greatest effort to drive out the invaders, he withdrew to his native

94 *Cong Abbey*

Connacht, high-king in name only. By the Treaty of Windsor, in October 1175, he recognised Henry II as his overlord, while he himself was recognised in turn as high-king of the parts of Ireland still unconquered by the Normans.

Ruairi O'Connor died in 1198 in the abbey at Cong to which he had retired, old and feeble, some years before. His death is recorded in the *Book of Leinster*: 'Ruairi died as a pilgrim in Cong.' He was buried at Clonmacnoise.[9]

It was the end of an era.

95 Clonmacnoise

16
Henry

With Dublin safely in Norman hands and the Irish national army routed, Strongbow turned his attention southwards – to Wexford, first, where Robert FitzStephen had been tricked into leaving his fort at Ferrycarrig and surrendering to the Norse. On their way to Wexford the Normans were harried and ambushed in Kildare and Carlow. In one skirmish Meiler FitzHenry was unhorsed by a blow of a stone.[1] In retaliation a monk named Nichol on the Norman side killed O Riain, the leader of the Irish ambushers, with a well-placed arrow. When they saw their leader fall the rest of the Irish broke and fled.

On the approach of Strongbow, the Norse-Irish occupants who had retaken Wexford from the Normans abandoned it and took refuge on Begerin Island in Wexford Harbour. They took FitzStephen with them as a hostage to be used in future negotiations, and from the sanctuary of Begerin sent Strongbow and Maurice FitzGerald a message that, if the Normans dared to attack the island, they would send back the severed head of FitzStephen to his half-brother Maurice.

Placing a new garrison in Wexford, the earl and FitzGerald next marched to Waterford which they reoccupied. Strongbow then proceeded against the irrepressible MacGiolla Phadraig of Ossory and was joined in this expedition by his brother-in-law Donal O'Brien, king of Limerick (Strongbow and Donal were married to daughters of Dermot MacMurrough).

MacGiolla Phadraig asked for a safe conduct through the Norman lines to Strongbow with whom he wished to negotiate, and the chivalrous Fleming and former ally of the Ossory king, Maurice de Prendergast, was deputed to see him safely to the earl. But on meeting Strongbow, MacGiolla Phadraig was charged with treason against the late king of Leinster, and O'Brien and his captains called for his death by hanging. Maurice de Prendergast, honourable to his word, sprang to the defence of the Ossorian and dared anyone to lay a hand on him. Strongbow, apparently influenced by Maurice's loyalty, ordered him to see MacGiolla Phadraig safely to his own side. We are told that Maurice lodged that night in the woods with the Ossorians and returned to Strongbow the next morning.

Shortly after this Murchadh MacMurrough came to terms with Earl Richard who granted him Uí Ceinnsealaigh while Donal Cavanagh was granted 'the pleas of Leinster' or jurisdiction over the Irish of the province.

Strongbow was now in full control of Leinster and the strongholds of Dublin, Waterford and Wexford. It was at this juncture that King Henry II stepped in.

Henry had, as early as July 1171, soon after the capture of Dublin by the Normans, heard all about the success attending Strongbow's expedition and feared the setting up of a rival Norman state in Ireland. At a council of his barons in the Normandy town of Argentan, he won their approval for an invasion of Ireland, no doubt producing the papal bull *Laudabiliter* and perhaps stressing that some of the Irish themselves wished him to come over.

There was another reason: Henry, at this time, needed a diversion from the unwelcome publicity attaching to the murder of Thomas Becket towards the end of 1170, for which he had been blamed. Pope Alexander III had called upon him to do public penance. An expedition to Ireland to curb the barbarous Irish would be just the thing to mollify the pope!

Henry's real intent, of course, was to curb the marauding Normans. He crossed from Normandy to Portsmouth and began his march across England to Gloucestershire where, at his orders, a great army was mobilising. At Winchester some surprising visitors waited on him – Murchadh MacMurrough (Dermot's brother) and representatives of the Norsemen of Wexford, with the news that they held as prisoner 'the felon' FitzStephen. MacMurrough and the Norsemen may have hoped to worm their way into Henry's good graces by this action and Henry, in turn, by promising to deal sternly with FitzStephen later, was anxious to give the impression to the Irish that he was their friend and protector.

When Henry reached his army's marshalling grounds at Newent, near Gloucester, he had another visitor – Strongbow himself. The earl had been summoned by Henry to England and he now appeared before his monarch and, according to Giraldus, they were reconciled after much altercation. The intermediary was Hervey de Monte Marisco who had carried Strongbow's earlier offer of the surrender of his Irish conquests to Henry. Now Strongbow repeated his submission and surrender and apparently placated the king. In return for his submission Henry granted Strongbow all of Leinster, except Dublin, its neighbouring coastal cantreds and the other ports and fortresses, to hold under the crown.[2]

These matters finally settled, Henry led his army to Pembroke where, at Milford Haven, on 6 October 1171, he and his men embarked in 400 ships (some accounts say 240) and sailed for Ireland. Henry's army, by the standards of those days, was a large and well-equipped one. It consisted of 500 knights and 4,000 men-at-arms and archers, with huge stocks of provisions and much equipment, such as tools, wooden assault towers, horses and spare arms and armour. Paradoxically, while this army ostensibly was an army of conquest, it did not have to loose a single arrow to achieve victory for Henry. By

96 Pembroke Castle

astute statesmanship and clever conciliation he won the submission of awed Irish and rebellious Normans alike – an astonishing bloodless conquest in the circumstances.

On 17 October, this largest invading force to date landed at Crook, on the western side of Waterford harbour.[3] The *Annals of the Four Masters* note the event: 'Henry the Second, king of England, duke of Normandy, earl of Anjou, and lord of many other countries, came to Ireland this year with a fleet of 240 ships, and landed at Waterford.'

The following day Henry and his army entered Waterford, where Strongbow formally surrendered the town to him and did homage for Leinster. Henry in return formally granted the kingdom of Leinster to the earl, with the exception of Dublin, Waterford and Wexford; these centres, with a coastal strip extending south of Dublin to Arklow, the king kept for himself. He also granted a special charter to the Norse of Waterford and took them under the protection of the Crown, as they had not resisted him.

To Waterford then came the Norse of Wexford, bringing with them Robert FitzStephen, in chains, whom they delivered to Henry. Giraldus says the king, in their presence, roundly condemned FitzStephen for being so presumptuous as to invade Ireland and to set up a separate Norman state there. To show he was the master Henry consigned the unfortunate FitzStephen to another prison, this time Reginald's Tower in Waterford. He was not to remain there for very long, of course.

There followed the extraordinary submission of most of the Irish kings and the whole Irish hierarchy to Henry. The submission of the Norman invaders of 1169 and 1170, who, after all, were Henry's own subjects, was to be expected, especially when it appeared that the king's anger at their earlier actions was largely simulated, and that many of them would be confirmed in their earlier grants of lands.

It is not so easy to understand why the independent-minded kings of Ireland meekly submitted, one by one, to a foreign king. Their action, and that of the Irish Church, must be viewed in the light of Henry's deliberate adoption of the role of protector, who had come to Ireland to save them from the marauding barons. But behind Henry's display as protector and benefactor, there stood the might of his well-equipped army – and well the Irish knew what well-armed, disciplined Normans could achieve on the field of battle!

The submission of the Irish hierarchy is also explainable. If they were not already aware of the papal approval for Henry's visitation, they were soon informed of it.

Thus, even before Henry left Waterford for what was to become a triumphal progress through the country, the first of the Irish kings had submitted. This was Dermot MacCarthy, of Desmond, who came, took an oath of

97 William the Conqueror granting lands

fealty, gave hostages and agreed to pay a yearly tribute. In return Henry gave him back his own kingdom of Desmond!

This ceremony was to be repeated again and again as Henry moved from Waterford to Lismore, thence to Cashel, back to Waterford and finally to Dublin.

Henry had a purpose in visiting Lismore where the bishop of the time was Christian O Conarchy. Christian was also papal legate and Henry's object in calling on him was probably to arrange for a synod of the Irish bishops. Similarly his visit to Cashel was undoubtedly made with the express purpose of meeting Archbishop Donal O hUallachain and to arrange for the holding of the synod there. In the midst of dealing with insubordinate Normans and submissive Irish, Henry pushed ahead with the most important part of his plan – the winning over of the native hierarchy by disclosing Pope Adrian's wishes for reform as outlined in *Laudabiliter*, and by underlining his own anxiety to set such reform in motion.

With plans for the convening of the council of bishops under way, Henry returned to Waterford, where he quietly released Robert FitzStephen, then commenced his slow march to Dublin. On the way, according to Giraldus, Henry sent Hugh de Lacy and William FitzAudelin as envoys to meet Ruairi O'Connor at Athlone, where the high-king submitted, as had other Irish kings – Dermot McCarthy, king of Desmond; Donal O'Brien, king of Thomond; Donal MacGiolla Phadraig, prince of Ossory; Melaghlin O Faolain of the Decies; Murchadh O'Carroll, king of Arighialla; Tiernan O'Rourke, prince of Breifne; MacFaelain of north Kildare; Donal MacGillamocholmog of south Dublin, and O'Toole, king of south Kildare. Some of the annals, notably those of Ulster, Lough Cé and Tighernach, omit mention of Connacht (Ruairi's kingdom) when listing the territories which submitted to Henry. The *Annals of the Four Masters* make no mention whatever of any submission by the Irish to Henry.

The Abbé MacGeoghegan says Ruairi and the envoys 'spent the time in paying mutual compliments'.[4] We may take it that Ruairi did not formally submit to Henry as high-king though he may, as inferred by Hanmer, have pledged the peace of Connacht.[5]

Alone of all the kingdoms of Ireland, the Cenél Eoghain

and Cénel Conaill in mid and west Ulster did not submit to Henry; they were, in fact, too remote to bother the king or be bothered by him. 'Thus,' says Hanmer, 'was all Ireland, save Ulster, brought under subjection.'

The submission of the Irish kings did not, however, mean as much as historians, particularly English ones, would have us believe. They were merely substituting one overlord for another, retaining full possession of and jurisdiction over their original territories and paying tributes to Henry which were no heavier than those they formerly paid to the Irish high-king.

For the moment they were happy to give homage to the overlord who promised to protect them from the rapacity of the Norman invaders. Soon these Irish subkings were to see the Irish bishops submit to Henry in an even more definite manner.

Henry reached Dublin on 11 November and took up residence in a specially constructed palace built of wattles, on the site of the Norse Thing-mote outside the walls.[6] Here, in sumptuous state, over Christmas 1171 and up to the beginning of February 1172, Henry received and entertained the Irish kings and chieftains and sent them back to their crude strongholds duly awed and impressed.

To Dublin itself Henry also gave new life. He drew up a charter, Dublin's first (which is still in existence in the municipal archives), by which he granted the city to his men of Bristol, to replace the original Norse inhabitants who had either been killed or had fled before the Norman occupiers. The granting of this charter was but one of the many acts of government which Henry performed during his sojourn. He set about the reorganisation of Irish society in the occupied territories along feudal lines, appointing officials and setting up a new legal and legislative system as he had done in England.

Meanwhile, at the council of prelates of the Irish Church which had convened at Cashel at Henry's comm-

98 Henry's II Charter to Dublin

and during the winter of 1171-72, the process of reform in the religious field was also receiving fresh attention, though as we have seen earlier, Church reform was well advanced in Ireland by the time of the Norman invasion.[7] The Irish bishops may have welcomed the impetus now added by such an illustrious personage as Henry, acting on the pope's instructions.

At any rate the synod of Cashel enacted a set of decrees which, briefly, enforced the payment of tithes, regulated the manner of catechising and baptism, laid down the Roman law for the contraction and observance of lawful marriages, decreed the freedom of the Church from secular imposts and enacted that divine offices would henceforth be celebrated in Ireland according to the forms and usages of the English Church.

Strangely enough, no mention seems to have been made of Pope Adrian's bull *Laudabiliter* at this synod, although its contents may have been privately commun-

99 Cashel

icated to the bishops assembled. This would go a long way towards explaining their readiness to submit to Henry and to co-operate with him in his reforms.

But we should also recall that Henry was, at this time, out of favour with the pope owing to the murder of Thomas Becket and, under the circumstances, would not have wished to draw further attention to himself by promulgating a bull issued by a previous pope. He took good care, however, to get each of the bishops to write a letter of submission, confirming to him and his heirs the kingdom of Ireland, and these letters Henry sent off to Pope Alexander III. His object, no doubt, was to curry favour with the papacy in order to obtain confirmation of Adrian's original grant. As we know, Alexander did issue a confirmatory brief which, with Adrian's *Laudabiliter*, was publicly promulgated at another synod in Waterford in 1175.

With Ireland subjugated Henry, restless as ever and anxious now for news from his other realms, prepared to leave for England. He left Dublin about the beginning of February 1172, and travelled to Wexford, where he planned to take ship for Wales. But adverse winds kept him in that town from the beginning of March to 17 April.

During his stay in Wexford he received some disquieting news from England: he was threatened with an interdict unless he returned immediately to meet the papal legates who had been seeking his reparation for Becket's murder; further, his own son Henry was organising a rebellion in England, backed by some of the more turbulent barons.

Tradition says that King Henry did penance for Becket's murder in the church at Selskar in Wexford at this time. He may have made the adjoining chapter-house his headquarters while in the town and from there issued the last edicts and grants of his Irish visitation.

These final arrangements were aimed, according to Giraldus, at 'strengthening his own party and weakening

100 Selskar Abbey

that of Earl Richard'. Henry, apparently, was still sus-
picious and wary of Strongbow and the early settlers.
Thus, while he confirmed Strongbow in the kingdom of
Leinster, he granted Meath (at which the kings of Leinster
had often cast covetous eyes) to Hugh de Lacy 'to hold as
Murchadh O Maolsheachlann or any other before or after
him had best held it'. Henry thus made certain that
Strongbow would be unable to claim Meath later on.

De Lacy was also appointed justiciar (king's representative) and constable of Dublin – in this also Henry
passed over Strongbow in favour of his own man. And to
make sure that none of the Geraldines or 'race of Nesta'
caused him any more trouble he placed such knights as
Robert FitzStephen, Maurice FitzGerald, Meiler FitzHenry
and Miles FitzDavid in the garrison of Dublin under
Hugh de Lacy. He similarly garrisoned Waterford and
Wexford with trusted men. Two other suspect Normans,
Raymond le Gros and Milo de Cogan, were seconded to

Henry's own personal retinue and left Ireland with the king.

Thus, after a visit of only six months, Henry laid the foundations of English rule in Ireland. On Easter Monday 17 April 1172, King Henry II sailed from Wexford, his army having left from Waterford on the previous day. Whatever plans he had in mind for the further control and administration of Ireland were never fulfilled, for he never returned to his newest realm.

101 Hugh de Lacy

17
Aftermath

Henry's departure from Ireland seemed to have been the signal awaited by his barons to renew their offensive. The fact was that, far from settling matters, Henry's grants to men like de Lacy were actually the cause of new turmoil, conflict between English and Irish interests being inevitable.

The first example of this conflict, and its results, can be found in the fate of the old die-hard Tiernan O'Rourke, king of Breifne. O'Rourke's claim on the ancient kingdom of Meath, now granted to de Lacy, dated from the division of that area in 1169. De Lacy's claim was naturally disputed by O'Rourke, who resisted manfully. Eventually a meeting between the two was arranged at the Hill of Ward, near Athboy.

What transpired is related in the *Annals of Ulster*:

> Tiernan O'Rourke, king of Breifne and Conmaicne, a man of great power for a long time, was killed by the Saxons and by Donal, son of Annadh O'Rourke of his own clan along with them. He was beheaded also by them, and his head and body were carried ignominiously to Dublin. The head was raised over the door of the fortress – a sore, miserable sight for the Gael. The body was hung in another place with the feet upwards.

Thus died, by treachery and at the hands of a member of his own clan, one of the central characters in our narrative – the man whose personal feud with Dermot MacMurrough had brought turmoil for so long to the land and, in the end, resulted in Dermot's flight for aid to Wales.

Donal O'Farrell of Conmaicne was the next native chieftain to be removed. His territory (approximating to part of the modern county of Longford) was also taken over by de Lacy.

Another Irish chieftain who was removed in the same year (1172) was Murchadh MacMurrough, brother of the late Dermot. His death at the hands of 'the English' removed a possible claimant for the kingdom of Leinster, now held by Strongbow.

Elsewhere and from now on other Irish kings and chieftains suffered the same fate as the Normans extended their greedy mailed claws into the south, west and north of the country. The conquest was halted momentarily in the spring of 1173 when both Strongbow and de Lacy were summoned by Henry for military service in Normandy. In their absence William FitzAudelin was sent over to Ireland to take charge.

But by September, Strongbow, with Raymond le Gros as his assistant, was back in Ireland as chief of state. He found most of the Irish leaders in arms against the Normans and set about 'pacifying' the country again. He marched into Munster, the seat of the rebellion, had some successes at first but, having lost his most energetic and experienced lieutenant Raymond (who had returned to Wales for his father's funeral), he was defeated by a powerful Irish alliance near Thurles in 1174. After this Strongbow withdrew to Waterford, probably chastened by the new turn of events. It was during this excursion into Munster that the ecclesiastical centre at Lismore was plundered by the Normans, an act which not only turned Donal O'Brien, king of Thomond and old ally of Dermot MacMurrough, against the Normans, but also, according to Giraldus, had a strange sequel. Those involved – Robert FitzStephen, Raymond le Gros, John de Courcy and Meiler FitzHenry – never had any lawful issue, 'a strange fatality,' says Giraldus, 'linked with the violation of the sanctuary lands at Lismore'.

The news of the defeat of the invaders near Thurles seems to have given the Irish new hope. 'All the people of Ireland with one consent rose against the English.'[1] Strongbow, besieged near Waterford, sent for aid to Raymond le Gros, who arrived at Wexford with about 450 men, relieved Earl Richard and conducted him to Wexford. Here Raymond married the earl's sister Basilia, who had been promised to him for the aid he had brought her brother.

Meanwhile de Lacy had been proceeding with the sub-infeudation of Meath (granting land as fiefs to his followers). It was the manner in which Strongbow, de Lacy, John de Courcy in Ulster, FitzStephen and Milo de Cogan in Munster, conquered and held these vast tracts of territory.

In Meath de Lacy parcelled out the land to his followers: Hugh Tyrell getting Castleknock; Gilbert de Angulo (or Nangle), Morgallion; Jocelin, son of Gilbert Nangle, Navan and Ardbracan; William de Missett, Lune; Adam Phepoe, Skrine, Santry and Clonturk; Gilbert

102　Carlingford Castle

FitzThomas, Kenlis; Hugh de Hose (Hussey), Deece; Gilbert de Nugent, Delvin; Richard Tuite, large tracts in Westmeath and Longford; Robert de Lacy, Rathwire; Meiler FitzHenry, Magherarnan, Rathherin and Athinorker; the Flemings, Slane, and so on.

As these lands were taken over, the Normans built their protective strongpoints and castles, established towns, founded abbeys – and prevailed on the Irish to stay and herd the cattle and till the land. In most instances this scheme succeeded. In any case the common people could do little but remain and do the bidding of their new masters; it was the native chiefs who suffered the loss of their territories and of the tribute paid by the lower orders.

If we have followed the fortunes of men like Strongbow, FitzStephen, de Cogan and FitzGerald, it is because they were the original invaders whose careers cover a particular era of the invasion. Their dream of an independent Norman state in Ireland had been shattered by King Henry; now they endeavoured to salvage what they could in the scramble for lands and riches. What they could not get by royal grant they strove to conquer by the

103 *Trim Castle*

104 Dunbrody Abbey

sword – and generally succeeded.

Maurice FitzGerald, who had obtained lands in County Kildare, spent his old age in his castle at Wicklow but died in Wexford in September 1176. He was buried in the abbey of the Grey Friars which no longer exists. He was seventy-five and his death came 'to the great grief of his friends', according to Giraldus. From him, however, sprang two great Geraldine families, the FitzGeralds of Leinster and of Desmond.

Robert FitzStephen was granted lands in Counties Cork and Kerry, which he had to win by the sword. His death is not recorded but some annals say he was killed along with Milo de Cogan in 1182.[2]

Raymond le Gros fought in many campaigns both in Ireland and abroad, and succeeded his uncle, FitzStephen, in his holdings in Cork before dying some time about 1186.[3]

Meiler FitzHenry lived to be appointed justiciar of

105 Tintern Abbey

Ireland in 1201. He held the post until 1208 when he fell from favour. About 1216 he entered a religious order and his lands in Leinster and Meath returned to the Crown since he had no son to succeed him. Other possessions in central Kerry passed to the Munster Geraldines when he died in 1220.

Hervey de Monte Marisco married Nesta, daughter of Maurice FitzGerald, but had no legitimate children. He was granted Bargy, in south County Wexford, by Earl Richard after the first landings. In 1171 he founded and endowed St Mary's Abbey, Dunbrody, and in 1179 he himself became a monk in the abbey of the Holy Trinity at Canterbury, to which he had given all his lands in County Wexford previously. These lands were later transferred to the abbey of Tintern, on an inlet of Bannow Bay. Hervey is said to be buried at Dunbrody.

Strongbow himself died in Dublin, in 1176, of a mortification in his foot. The *Annals of the Four Masters*,

106 Dundrum Castle (top): 107 Carrickfergus Castle

recording his death, say: 'Strongbow died of an ulcer in his foot, a visitation attributed to Saints Bridget, Columkille and other saints, whose churches he had destroyed, and it is said that he thought he saw St Bridget killing him.' The earl was buried in Christ Church, Dublin, with Archbishop Laurence O'Toole performing the obsequies.[4] By his Irish wife Aoife he had a son who died in infancy and a daughter Isabel.[5] She later married William le Mareschal, earl marshal of Ireland, who succeeded through this marriage to Strongbow's possessions in Leinster and the earldom of Pembroke in Wales.

By 1190, then, Strongbow, FitzStephen, de Cogan, Maurice FitzGerald and Raymond le Gros were all dead. So, too, was Hugh de Lacy, who was killed by an Irish worker while assisting at the building of a castle at Durrow in July 1186.[6]

After Strongbow's death, John de Courcy, who is listed by Camden among those who came to Ireland with Dermot in 1169, became the Norman 'strongman' and conquered Ulster in typically ruthless Norman fashion.

Orpen says de Courcy had fought for King Henry II both in England and in France in his war with the barons and may have accompanied Henry to Ireland in 1171. 'His story,' writes Orpen, 'is like a wild romance, and would hardly be believed were it not for many solid and enduring facts which testify to its essential truths. He is described as a tall fair man with big bones and muscular frame, of immense strength and remarkable daring. A born warrior, in action ever in the front, ever taking upon himself the brunt of the danger.' While in Ireland Henry granted him 'Ulster, if he could conquer it.' De Courcy did not hesitate about doing so. With a band of twenty-two men-at-arms and about 300 others, supplemented by some of the Irish themselves, he advanced into Ulster and took by surprise the town of Down, chief seat of the kings of Uladh. In a counter-attack, the then king, Mac Donlevy, tried to retake the seat but was badly beaten by de Courcy who then set about fortifying his position by erecting a great motte about a quarter of a mile from the cathedral city. From here he extended his sway over Uladh (now represented by Counties Down and Antrim) but had to fight many battles to hold on to his new possessions. In one of these encounters de Courcy's men captured croziers carried into battle by the archbishop of Armagh and the bishop of Down, the Book of Armagh and a sacred bell. The latter two 'noble relics' were later restored to the Irish.

Like other Norman knights, de Courcy consolidated his position by marrying well. His bride, whom he wed in 1180, was Affreca, daughter of Gottred, king of Man, a marriage aimed at strengthening an alliance with the Norse, who still lingered in some ports on the Irish mainland. When, in 1204, de Courcy was driven out of Uladh he was aided by Reginald, king of Man, his brother-in-law.

A great builder of castles and monasteries, de Courcy also introduced Benedictine monks, Cistercians and Crutched Friars into Uladh and in time became virtual prince of Ulster, with unlimited jurisdiction.

After Prince John's disastrous visit to Ireland in 1185, Henry turned to de Courcy, as one of his ablest administrators, and made him justiciar, a position de Courcy held until the start of the reign of Richard I (1189). He led expeditions into Munster and Connacht but, after a defeat in 1188, was superseded and retired to his lordship of Ulster. With the ascension to the throne of King John, de Courcy's days were numbered. He incurred John's anger, was ousted by the de Lacys (at the king's behest) in 1204, made a final attempt to regain his territories but failed. He was given permission to return to England in 1207 and became reconciled with the king. John apparently used him on his expedition to Ireland in 1210 and again when Louis of France was threatening Winchester in 1216. But de Courcy never regained either his power or his possessions in Ireland. He retired to a monastery in Chester and later returned to France, where he died in 1219.

With the passing of the old guard Henry felt free to give Ireland into the care of his son John who had been styled 'lord of Ireland', a title which denoted that Ireland was no longer regarded as a kingdom but as a feudal lordship. John arrived in Ireland in 1185 at the head of a new army, bringing with him many new settlers.[7]

Another phase in the Norman occupation had opened.

108 Emblems of the lordship of Ireland

18

Epilogue

By 1200 the foreigners had occupied territory east of a line roughly drawn from Antrim to Clones, then to Athlone and Limerick and south to Cork. West Ulster, Connacht and west Munster remained mostly unoccupied by the Normans, the native chieftains and kings having resisted or not yet been attacked. Their turn soon came.

Rev F. X. Martin writes:

By the year 1250 – within eighty years of the invasion – three-quarters of the country had been overrun by the Normans. Nobody has ever accused the Gaelic Irish of lack of courage, yet how account for the success of the Norman forces in Ireland? They were far less in numbers than the Irish, they were fighting far from their homes in England and Wales, they had little or no support from the king of England. It was each Norman for himself.

The Normans were not only a race of warriors but those who came to Ireland were seasoned fighters against the Welsh, whose tactics and weapons were much the same as those of the Irish. The Normans advanced into battle on an organised plan, unlike the Irish who bravely charged in disarray. The Normans, superior in their weapons – the long sword, the lance, the iron helmet, the hauberk of mail covering body, thigh and arms, contrasted with the Irish soldier carrying his axe and short sword, and clad in a linen tunic. One of the most feared groups of the invaders were the

Welsh archers with their cross-bows; the Irish spear, javelin and sling-stones, hitherto so effective, were no match for the far-flying arrows of the Welsh. What Irish army could stand the shock, first of a shower of deadly Welsh arrows, followed by a charge of armed Norman knights on horseback and completed by an onslaught from disciplined lines of Flemish foot-soldiers?[1]

Herein lay the explanation of Norman success on the field of battle. But apart from being skilled soldiers the Normans were also thorough colonisers. Having conquered a territory by the sword they set about colonising and administrating it – first by erecting defences on its perimeter and at other strategic points, then by parcelling out the land to their own followers to make use of it. The early Norman strong-points were mottes of earth and timber – not until the thirteenth century did the Normans commence to build their stone castles.

Within the occupied territories they planted the fertile

109 Castleknock Castle

110 Seal of King John

lands with their followers, each group of feudal tenants
under a knight in his castle or manor-house, the knights
in turn owing allegiance to the royal grantees. The colonisation of south Wexford, particularly the so-called
'English baronies' of Forth and Bargy, may be taken as a
fair example of the system at work. Strongbow granted
these two baronies to Hervey de Monte Marisco who
colonised his holdings with Norman, Flemish and Welsh
soldiers and followers, dividing the lands between the
Suttons, Prendergasts, Roches, Sinnotts, Rossiters, Fur-
longs, Hays, Keatings, Cheevers, Codds and others.

Mainly because of its rather isolated geographical position in Ireland and its proximity to the mother country of
Wales – and perhaps not a little due to the stout independence and courage of its inhabitants – this area has
maintained its unique Norman character to the present
day. In its numerous stone castles, well-tilled and tidy
farms, in the speech and habits of the people, even in their
appearance, this part of County Wexford is a living
reminder of the influence of the Normans.[2]

This warlike people also gave the country considerable
peaceful benefits. In the administrative field it was the
Normans who established centralised government in
Ireland – the much-maligned John, in fact, substituted

English law and order, based on the Magna Charta (1215), for feudal disorder. A jury system was introduced and sheriffs were appointed. A coinage for Ireland was struck.

The Normans were great builders and the remains of their castles and abbeys throughout the country testify to their skill and to the endurance of their materials. Settlements grew up round castles or strong-points, so most of the country's towns and villages were founded by the Normans and with the growth of towns there emerged a pattern of trade, domestic and foreign. Wealth followed trade.

Nor were the Normans entirely materialistic. Wherever they went, religious activity manifested itself, in new religious orders brought in from the Continent and from England, in new churches and abbeys which sprang up throughout the occupied territories. It is not easy to reconcile such activities with a fighting race. But J. C. Walsh, historian of the Walshes, has supplied an admirable explanation:

> There was one feature of this Norman civilisation in Ireland which at first sight is not easy to understand. These men who had no scruple whatever about taking what belonged to others, with whatever incidental slaughter was involved in the process, took advantage

111 Athassel Abbey

112 *Youghal Abbey*

of the first period of comparative peace to build an abbey. The first Theobald Butler built one at Owney, and was buried there. William de Burgh built one at Athassel, and was buried there. Maurice FitzGerald the Second founded an abbey at Youghal, and was buried there. Hervey de Monte Marisco founded an abbey at Dunbrody, and was buried there. The last two, after definitely deciding that they had had enough of worldly affairs, returned to their abbeys to await the call, and Hervey even became abbot, his effigy showing the knight's armour under the monk's cowl. As late as 1326, Richard de Burgh, the aged earl of Ulster, at a Parliament in Kilkenny, resigned his possessions to his grandson, took leave of his fellow nobles after sumptuously entertaining them, and retired to his monastery at Athassel where he ended his days. The first Fitz-Maurice of Kerry founded an abbey at Ardfert, and the crowning indignity offered to Thomas FitzMaurice in 1590 was the refusal of the English Viceroy to permit his burial in the tomb of his ancestors at this same abbey of Ardfert. John of Callan, husband of Margery Walsh, built an abbey at Tralee which became the burial place of the Desmonds. Meyler FitzHenry built and was buried in the abbey of Old Connell in Kildare. Raymond FitzWilliam was buried at Molana Abbey, on the Blackwater. The first settlers vied with one another in endowing the abbey of St Thomas à Becket, though they were soldiers of King Henry II, who was to blame for his martyrdom. Geoffrey FitzRobert built the abbey of Kells, and he and his neighbour, Matthew FitzGriffin, richly endowed it. Thomas FitzAnthony built the abbey of Inistioge.

Some Irish writers are rather cynical in their comments on all this, describing it as a more or less hypocritical attempt at penitential reparation. But that explanation evidently is not conclusive. It might be nearer the truth to assume that the career of arms, to

113 Kells

these men, trained as they were, represented the highest conception of honourable achievement. They were no more ashamed of it, nor of the incidence of its prosecution, than a modern captain of industry is ashamed of competition in business. To meet and defeat an enemy was for them part of a day's work; it did not diminish, and it may have increased, their concern for the problem of eternity.[3]

Compare this attitude with that of the fighter-pilot in the most recent world war who, from the cockpit of his deadly machine, 'reached out, and touched the face of God'.

Turbulent and warlike though they were, the Normans did not engage in fighting just for fighting's sake. Conversely they often brought peace in their train.

Rev F. X. Martin writes:

It would be a mistake to think of Norman Ireland as engaged in continuous deadly warfare with the Gael. Once an area was occupied by the Normans it gained peace and order, where previously there had been raids and counter-raids between warring factions of the great Gaelic families. It is true that war continued in the border areas between the Gael and Gall, but that was no fiercer than the clash of arms within the Gaelic terri-

114 Molana Abbey

tories between different Gaelic territories, between different Gaelic families or various members of the same family. Contrast the organised land of peace in Leinster, Meath and much of Munster with the turbulent condition of Connacht under the O'Connors.[4]

Orpen agrees with this view: 'Less than half a century from the time when the first invader set foot in Ireland, it is, I think, manifest that the most prominent effect of the Anglo-Norman occupation was not, as has been represented, an increase of turmoil, but rather the introduction over large tracts of Ireland of a measure of peace and prosperity quite unknown before.'[5]

It was a measure of peace, certainly, but it was peace at a price. The Irish common people were vassals, the Irish chiefs dispossessed in many cases of their best lands, and the old Irish system, with all its faults, was slowly being extinguished. With the growth and extension of Anglo-Norman power in Ireland and the forging of link after link in the chain binding the two islands together, the chances faded of a Norman-Irish state emerging. This was the great tragedy of the entire adventure. The two peoples had so much in common that a harmonious and successful blending would have been inevitable. (As it was, it took many years of war and legislation to counter the natural amalgamation of Gael and Norman that actually took place.) This began with the taking of Irish wives by many of the invaders – Aoife by Strongbow; Rose O'Connor, daughter of High-King Ruairi, by Hugh de Lacy; a daughter of Donal O'Brien of Thomond by William de Burgh. It progressed with the military alliances between Norman knights and Irish chieftains – those of Maurice de Prendergast with Donal MacGiolla Phadraig and of Strongbow with Donal Cavanagh are examples.

A common religion laid the foundations for further co-mingling of the two peoples. Intermarriage led to the adoption by the new generations of the Irish language, Irish names, Irish customs. Within two hundred years it became necessary for the Parliament at Kilkenny to pass the act called the 'Statutes of Kilkenny' (1366) which prohibited, under penalty of high treason, the families of Anglo-Normans settled in Ireland from forming any alliances or intermarriages with the native Irish, and the Norman-Irish from adopting Irish surnames, the Irish language, dress, manners or customs.

Why did the first Norman attempts to set up an independent state in Ireland fail? Largely because of the 'go-it-alone' attitude of the early invaders, then divisions in the Norman ranks, and, at a later stage, King Henry's stratagem of devolving power to his own hand-picked men rather than to the Strongbownians and Geraldines. There was also, of course, the stiffening of Irish opposition to Norman power.

Rev F. X. Martin writes:

> The tragedy of the Norman invasion was not the conquest of Ireland – for that never took place – but the half-conquest. The Normans never came in sufficient

numbers to complete the conquest while the kings of England, on whom rested the responsibility for the peace and progress of Ireland, were either too zealous to assist their barons in Ireland or too distracted by dangers in England and wars on the continent to turn their minds seriously to the Irish problem. If the conquest had been completed as in Normandy, England and Sicily, a new nation would have emerged, combining the qualities of both peoples. Instead, by the year 1300 there was a drawn battle, with the Normans controlling most of the country, but the tide was already beginning to turn against them. The Irish question had become part of the heritage of Ireland and of England.[6]

That heritage was to include, over the next six hundred and fifty years or so, war and bloodshed, pestilence and famine, shining bravery and hateful deceit. With that heritage we still live. It is ironic that while we remember the half-conquest and the conquest that might have been, the twin inheritors of the bloody heritage, Ireland and England, are even still engaged in battle – political and cultural – the outcome of which will undoubtedly mean the vanquishing of the weaker side. Will the conquest of Ireland be then finally achieved?

115 Limerick Castle

Norman and Anglo-Norman Names

This list of family names, largely drawn from personal research and from Edward MacLysaght's *The Surnames of Ireland* does not purport to be a definitive collection of Norman and Anglo-Norman surnames found in Ireland. The names listed appear to be the most common cognomens deriving from the Norman invasion and settlement of Ireland and the areas mentioned are those where the names are or were most commonly found. (*Note:* Fitz means *fils*, son).

Archbold (Anglo-Norman) – east Leinster and Wicklow.
Archer (Anglo-Norman) – Kilkenny.
Aylward, Elward – Waterford and Kilkenny.

Babe, from le Babbe (Anglo-Norman) – formerly Louth.
Bacon, from le Bacoun.
Baldwin – Waterford.
Barneville, Barnewall (Anglo-Norman) – The Pale.
Barrett – Munster and Connacht.
Barron, from le Baron – Wexford.
Barry – Cork and Wexford.
Beamish (Anglo-Norman) – Cork and Kerry.
Begg(e) – Leinster and Ulster.

Bellew, from de Belleau – Louth and Meath.
Belton, from de Weldon (Anglo-Norman) – The Pale.
Bermingham, Corish (Anglo-Norman) – Galway, Kildare and Wexford.
Berrill, Birrell – Louth.
Blanchfield, from de Blancheville – Kilkenny.
Bluett, Blewett – Cork and Limerick.
Blunt, from le Blound.
Bonfield, from de Bonneville – Limerick and Clare.
Bouchier, Boucher, Busher – Wexford, Cork and Waterford.
Boyce, Boyse, from Bois.
Breadon – Leinster.

Browne, from le Brun – Galway, Wexford, Limerick and Mayo.

Bryan, Brien – Kilkenny and Wexford.

Burke, from de Burgo – Connacht.

Burnell, from Brun – Meath, Dublin and Clare.

Bury.

Busher, *see* Bouchier.

Butler, from Boteler, Botiller, le Bottiller – Kilkenny and Tipperary.

Campion – Laois and Kilkenny.

Cantillon, Cantlin – Kerry.

Carew, from de Carron – Tipperary, Cork, Carlow and Mayo.

Cashell, from de Cashel (Anglo-Norman) – Louth and Thomond.

Chambers, from de la Chambre – Ulster and Mayo.

Cheevers, Chivers, from Chievre – Wexford.

Clare, Clear – Wexford and Kilkenny.

Codd, Codde, Cody – Wexford.

Cogan, Coogan – Cork.

Comyn (Hiberno-Norman) – Clare.

Condon, from Caunteton – Cork.

Courcy, de Courcy – Cork.

Croker, from le Cro(c)ker – Kilkenny.

116 Bermingham Castle

117 Butler coat of arms   *118 Browne coat of arms*

Cruise, from de Cruys –
   Meath and Dublin.
Cullen, Cullin – Wexford.
Curtis, from le Cuirteis – east
   Leinster and Wexford.
Cussen – Limerick, Cork and
   Wexford.

Dalton, from d'Alton – Clare.
Darcy, from d'Arci – Mayo,
   Galway and Wexford.
Dardis, from d'Ardis
   (Normandy or Puy-de-
   Dome) – Westmeath.
Daton, Doughton, from
   d'Auton – Kilkenny.
Day, from de Haye – Wexford.
Deane, from le Den/
   Denn/Denne – Dublin.
Delahyde – Dublin.
Delamer, from de la
   Mere/Mare – Dublin.
Denvir, from d'Anver – Down.
Devereux, Deverill, Devery,
   from d'Evreux – Wexford.

Dillon – Meath, Westmeath,
   Roscommon and Wexford.
Dondon, Dundon, from de
   Auno – Limerick.
Dowdall – The Pale.

Esmonde – Wexford.
Eustace – Kildare.
Everard (Anglo-Norman) –
   Meath and Tipperary.

Fagan – Dublin and Meath.
Fanning, Fannin – Limerick
   and Tipperary.
Fitzelle, Fizzell – Kerry and
   Antrim.
Fitzgerald – Kildare and Cork.
Fitzgibbon – Mayo and
   Limerick.
Fitzharris, Fitzhenry –
   Wexford. McHenry –
   Connacht.
Fitzjames, rare.
Fitzwilliam, Macwilliam,
   MacQuillan.

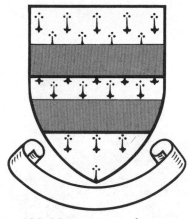

119 De Lacy coat of arms

120 Nugent coat of arms

Fitzmaurice – Kerry.
Fitzsimmons – Mayo, Cavan
 and Down.
Fitzstephens – Cork.
Flavelle – Armagh.
Forrestal – Kilkenny.
Francis, from le Franceis –
 Galway.
French, ffrench – Wexford
 and Galway.
Freyne, de Freyne – Kilkenny
 and Wexford.
Frizell, Frizelle, from le
 Friesian – Munster.
Furlong – Wexford.

Ganter, from le Ganter,
 glovemaker – Dublin.
Garland, Gernon, from de
 Gernon – Monaghan and
 Louth.
Gaskin, from Gascoigne –
 Leinster.
Gaynard, Gernon – Mayo and
 Monaghan.

Gerard, Gerrard.
Gilbert.
Glanville, Glanfield –
 Munster.
Gorham – Kerry.
Grace, from le Gros – Kilkenny.
Granfield, Granville – Kerry.
Grendon, Grindon, Grennon –
 Mayo and Monaghan.
Griffin, Griffith (Cambro-
 Norman) – Kilkenny.

Hackett – Kilkenny and
 Kildare.
Hadsor, rare – Louth and
 Dublin.
Hastings, Hestin.
Hay, Hayes, from de la Haye –
 Wexford.
Headon – Wexford.
Hendron, Henderson – Ulster.
Herbert – Kerry.
Hollywood – Dublin, Oriel.
Hore, from le Hore (Anglo-
 Norman) – Wexford.

121 Kilkenny Castle

Horsey.
Hosey, Hussey – Meath and
  Kerry
Howell.
Howlett, Howlin, Holden –
  Wexford.

Jordan (d'Exeter) – Connacht,
  Wexford

Keating (Cambro-Norman),
  from Cethyn – south
  Leinster.
Keirsey, Kiersey – Waterford.

Lacy, de Lacy, from de Lascy –
  Limerick and Wexford.
Laffan (Anglo-Norman) –
  Wexford and Tipperary.
Lambert, Lamport – Wexford
  Galway and Mayo.

Landy – Kilkenny and
  Tipperary.
Large.
Lawless – Dublin and Galway.
Liston, from de Lexinton –
  Limerick.
Logan, from de Logan.
Lucey, from de Lucy.
Lynch, from de Lench –
  Galway.
Lyvet – Leinster.

MacElligott, from Fitzelias,
  also Lyons – Kerry.
Mansfield, from de
  Mandeville, MacQuillan,
  MacWilliam, Cullen –
  Tipperary, Oriel and
  Waterford.
Marmion, Merriman – The
  Pale.

Marshall – Wexford and
  Ulster.
Maunsell, Mansell – Limerick,
  Tipperary and Wexford.
Mayler, Meyler, Myler –
  Wexford.
MacQuillan, MacWilliam, *see*
  Mansfield.
Melville – Ulster.
Miniter – Clare.
De Moleyns, Mullins.
Molyneux – Kerry and Ulster.
Montague, from de
  Montaigue – Tyrone and
  Armagh.
Mortimer – Meath.
Montmoreney, from de Monte
  Marisco.
Mountain, Mountaine, from
  de la Montagne –
  Waterford.

Nagle, Nangle, from d'Angulo
  – Cork and Sligo.
Netterville, Netterfield –
  Meath.
Neville – Wexford and
  Kilkenny.
Nicolls, Nicholas,
  MacNicholas, MacNicolls –
  Tyrone.
Noble, from le Noble –
  Fermanagh.
Nugent, from de Nogent –
  Westmeath and Cork.

Oliver – Ulster and Louth.

Palmer, from le Paumer (the
  pilgrim).

Pentony, Penthony – Meath,
  Louth and Dublin.
Peppard – Louth and
  Wexford.
Plunkett (Anglo-Norman) –
  Meath.
Power, from le Poer –
  Waterford and Wexford.
Prende(r)ville – Kerry.
Prendergast, Pender – Mayo,
  Tipperary and Wexford.
Prout, Proud – Ormond.
Punch – Kildare.
Purcell, Purtill – Tipperary
  and Clare.

Quilter, from le Cuilter
  (quiltmaker) – north Kerry.

Redmond – Wexford.
Roberts. Rochford, Ratchford,
  from de Ridelsford – Cork,
  Wexford, Meath and
  Kilkenny.
Rossiter (Anglo-Norman) –
  south Wexford.
Russell – Leinster and Ulster.

Scriven – Dublin and Cork.
Shortall.
St Leger – Cork and
  Waterford.
St John.
Savage – Ards Peninsula and
  Kilkenny.
Scales (Anglo-Norman) –
  Limerick and Clare.
Scurlock – Wexford.
Shinnors (Anglo-Norman) –
  Tipperary and Limerick.

Stacpoole, Stackpoole – Clare and Dublin.
Stafford – Wexford.
Stapleton – Kilkenny and Tipperary.
Staunton – Connacht.
Sutton – Wexford and Kildare.
Swayne – Leinster.

Taafe, Taaffe, Taffe – Louth and Sligo.
Talbot – Dublin.
Tallon – Leinster.
Teeling – Meath.
Tobin, from St. Aubyn – Leinster.
Tuite – Leinster.
Tyrrell – Westmeath.

Ussher – Dublin.
Veale – Waterford.
Verdon – Leinster.

Viniter, from le Vineter – Munster.

Wade – Waterford and Wexford.
Wall, Wale, from de Valle – Munster.
Wallace, from le Waleis (the Welshman), Scots – Irish.
Walsh, Walshe, Welsh – Wexford and Kilkenny.
Warren, from de la Varenne – The Pale.
Waring, from Guarin, later Warin – Meath, Kilkenny and Down.
White, from le Blanc, Blund – Down and Sligo.
Woulfe – Limerick and Kildare.
Wyse, from le Wyse (the wise man) – Waterford and Wexford.

Norman Flemish Names

Bolger – Wexford.
Boscher, Busher – Wexford. *see* also Bouchier.

Chievres, Cheevers, Chivers – Wexford.
Colfer – Wexford.
Connick – Wexford.
Cullen, Cullin – Wexford.
Cusac, Cusack.

Fleming – Meath.

Harford – Dublin and Kilkenny.

Parle – Wexford.

Roche, from FitzGodebert de la Roche – Wexford and Cork.

Siggin, Siggins – Wexford.
Sinnott, Synad – Wexford and Kildare.

Waddick – Wexford.
Wadding – South Wexford.
Whitty, from Whythay – Wexford.

Norse and Norse-Irish Names

Arthur, Arthurs.

Beirne, O'Birn, O'Beirn, from
    Norse Bjorn.
Blacker.
Bligh.
Bolan.
Broder, Broderick, Broaders.
Burney, Birney, from Mac
    Biorna.

Caskey, MacAskie.
Coll.
Coppinger.
Cotter, from MacOitir.
O'Cottle.

Dolphin.

O'Goherig, from Gothfrith.

Harold.
Hendrick, Henrick (Cambro-
    Norse).
Hever.

MacIvor, Iver – Tyrone.

Jennings, from Jen or Jan.

Kettle – Dublin and Louth.

MacLoughlin, from Mac
    Lochlainn.
MacManus.

Neilson, Nelson, from Njall.

Sigerson.

Skiddy – Cork.
Skiller, Skilling – Down.
MacSorley – Tyrone and
    Antrim.
Storey – Ulster and Dublin.
Sugrue, from Shrugue.
Sweetman, from Svatman –
    Kilkenny and Wexford.
MacSwiggan, from Swegen,
    Swen.

Thunder – Louth and Dublin.
Toner, Tonry – Ulster.
(O) Torney – midlands.
Trant.
Tuke, from Chooke, Tooke.

122 *Roche coat of arms*

Sources and Notes

Foreword

1 In the preface to his monumental work, *Ireland under the Normans* (Oxford, 1911, 1920; repr. 1968), Goddard H. Orpen says that the Norman invasion was 'the most far-reaching event that occurred in Ireland since the introduction of Christianity'

2 Preface to *Ireland under the Normans*, vol. I. Though Orpen was referring here to the Norse invasion, his remarks could equally apply to the Norman threat

1 Sources

1 W. Llewelyn Williams, Introduction to *Itinerary* and *Description of Wales* by Giraldus Cambrensis (J. M. Dent, 1908)

2 Reginald Poole, *Social England*, vol. I, p. 342

3 Kate Norgate, *England under the Angevin Kings*, vol. II, p 457

4 Translated from the original Latin by Theophilus O'Flanagan of Trinity College (1795). Joly Pamphlets collection, National Library, Dublin

5 *Patrician Decad.* Referred to in *Cambrensis Eversus* by Gratianus Lucius (Dr John Lynch)

6 The particular version of Gerald's account of the invasion upon which I have drawn here is *The Historical Works of Giraldus Cambrensis, Containing the History of the Conquest of Ireland*, translated by Thomas Forester and revised and edited by Thomas Wright (George Bell & Son, London, 1881)

7 Preface, *Ireland under the Normans*, vol. I. Orpen, in my opinion, is being a little too generous in his praise of Gerald here. But it is difficult to be overcritical of such an extraordinary character

8 The Carew manuscript in the Archiepiscopal Library at

Lambeth Palace, London. Todd's catalogue of manuscripts in the library has this entry: An old French metrical Fragment containing the first three years of the Conquest of Ireland. At the beginning is the following note, in a modern hand: 'This old Fragment wants both the beginning & ending. Nevertheless, in the first ten lines, it appears that this Story was written by one called Maurice Regan (sometimes mentioned in this discourse), who was servant and interpreter unto Dermond Mac Moroghe king of Leinster, & put into French meeter by one of his familiar acquaintance. It endeth abruptly with the winning of Limerick, which was not full 3 years after Robert Fitz Stephen's first arrival in Ireland'

9 It is Orpen's translation, which he also edited and footnoted, that I draw on for this book (Oxford, 1892)
10 Introduction, *The Song of Dermot and the Earl*
11 Historical criticism of *The Song of Dermot and the Earl*, *Irish Historical Studies*, vol. I, no. 1 (Hodges Figgis, Dublin, March 1938)

2 Bridgeheads

1 O'Curry, *Manuscript Materials of Ancient Irish History*
2 Gabriel O'C. Redmond, 'History and Topography of the Parish of Hook', *Journal of the Waterford and South-East Ireland Archaeological Society*, vol. V
3 Philip H. Hore, 'History of the Barony of Forth, The Past', nos. 1 2, 3 and 5 (Uí Ceinnsealaigh Historical Society, Wexford, 1920 *et seq*)
4 'History and Topography of the Parish of Hook'
5 The unusual part played by Milford Haven in Irish history is worth noting. From here Patrick was taken, an event that led to the christianisation of Ireland, from here most of the Norman invaders took ship for their attempt to conquer Ireland, and it was to Milford Haven that the gun-running *Asgard* called on her voyage from Hamburg to Howth in 1914 – three significant milestones in our history
6 The terms 'Norsemen' and 'Vikings' now appear interchangeable, though the earlier incursions are usually attributed to Norsemen *per se*
7 *Book of Rights*, a modified form of which is preserved in the fourteenth-century *Book of Ballymote*
8 'History and Topography of the Parish of Hook'

9 Miscellaneous Annals
10 *Ireland under the Normans*, chap. I, vol. I
11 *Ireland under the Normans*, chap. I, vol. I
12 Preface to *Ireland under the Normans*

3 Turmoil

1 *Annals of Lough Cé*, vol. I, p. 7
2 Uí Ceinnsealaigh, often rendered Hy Kinsella, was Mac-
   Murrough country
3 Mary Hayden and George A. Moonan, *A Short History of the
   Irish People* (Dublin and Cork), part I, chap II, p. 13
4 *Annals of Clonmacnoise* and *Book of Leinster*
5 T.W. Moody and F. X. Martin (eds), *The Course of Irish
   History* (Cork, 1984), chap. VII, p. 116
6 *Annals of Lough Cé* and *of Ulster*
7 *Ireland under the Normans*, vol. I, p. 50
8 *Annals of the Four Masters*
9 *Book of Leinster*
10 *The Course of Irish History*, chap. VII, p. 121
11 *Annals of the Four Masters*

4 Abduction

1 *Annals of Tighernach*. This title is given to a lacunose manuscript, mainly containing entries for the years 489-766 and
   974-1178, and which is named after Tighernach, abbot of
   Clonmacnoise who died in 1088. The *Annals* are found in a
   fourteenth-century manuscript now in the Bodleian Library,
   Oxford (MS Rawlinson B.488)
2 *Book of Leinster*. But O'Donovan, in the *Annals of the Four
   Masters* (1052), says Dermot was 62 in 1153, which would
   put his birth at 1090. This also would mean that he was just
   eighty in 1171, up to which time he had been extremely
   active and vigorous – exceptional in a man of eighty. Arthur
   Ua Clerigh (*The History of Ireland to the Coming of Henry II*,
   London, vol. I, p. 395) suggests that the entry in the *Book of
   Leinster* which we quote above should read LXXI (71) and
   not LXI (61). 'Mistakes often occur in Roman numerals,' he
   adds
3 *Expugnatio Hibernica*
4 *Annals of Ulster* (1127), *Annals of Lough Cé* (1132), and *Annals
   of Clonmacnoise* (1135)

5 *Ireland under the Normans*, vol. I, p. 44
6 *Book of Leinster*. Eanna is believed to have been illegitimate as well. 'Nor is it quite clear,' writes Ua Clerigh (*The History of Ireland*, vol. I, p. 400), 'that Eva (Aoife) was legitimate. If so her younger sister was married before her to O'Brien, which would be against the invariable usage of the Gael'
7 Geoffrey Keating, *Foras Feasa ar Eirinn*, book II, p. 319
8 *Foras Feasa ar Eirinn*, book II, p. 319
9 *Foras Feasa ar Eirinn*, book II
10 *Annals of the Four Masters*, *Annals of Tighernach*, and *Annals of Clonmacnoise* (1152)
11 *Ireland under the Normans*, vol. I, p. 56
12 I have seen it stated (in *The Geraldines* by Brian FitzGerald, Staples Press, 1951) that Dervorgilla bore Dermot a daughter. She may have been the 'Dervorgil' who married Donal MacGiollamocholmog
13 *Annals of Tighernach* (1153)
14 *Annals of Tighernach* (1157)
15 Arthur Ua Clerigh, *The History of Ireland*, vol. I, p. 313

5 Exile

1 'This abominable practice of blinding had come west from the east, and was common in England from the time of the Conquest, as well as in Ireland.' Ua Clerigh, *The History of Ireland*, vol. I, p. 397
2 *Ireland under the Normans*, vol. I, p. 63
3 Rev Dr J. F. O'Doherty, *Irish Historical Studies*, vol. I, no. 2 (1938)
4 *MacCarthaigh's Book* in Miscellaneous Irish Annals (AD 1114-1437), translated and edited by Seamus O hInnse (1947), says, however, that Ruairi and his allies 'burned Fearna Mhor Maodhog (Ferns), with all its churches'. This book also claims that Ruairi returned on the second hosting against Dermot when 'he demolished MacMurchadha's stone house and they banished himself eastwards oversea to the king of England (who was) in France'. Also *Book of Leinster*.
    MacCarthaigh's Book is so called because the owner was Finghin MacCarthaigh Mor (c.1562-1640), an Irish chieftain who spent many years in English hands, between imprisonment in the Tower and detention in London. He was a noted scholar who employed scribes to make compilations for him

5 *Book of Leinster*
6 Afterwards called 'Murchadh na nGael' to distinguish him from Diarmuid na nGall
7 A letter copied into the *Book of Leinster*, from Finn MacGorman to Aodh, directs that the conclusion of the *Book* be written by Aodh. Finn died in 1160. (*See* chap. 1)
8 *The Song of Dermot.* Orpen (*Journal of the Royal Society of Antiquaries of Ireland*, 1903, vol. XXXIII, p. 418) identifies *Corkeran* with *Gort Corcoran* or *Corkcorgraine* near Youghal, County Cork, maintaining that Dermot could not get a ship at any nearer place. William H. Grattan Flood disputes this (*Journal RSAI*, 1904, vol. XXXIV, part II, pp. 191-2), holding that 'the natural place whence Dermot most likely set sail ought to be sought in County Wexford only, and he locates 'Corkeran' at 'Corkerry', at Great Island near New Ross.

Neither of them seems to have given any thought to the possibility that since Bannow Bay was the first landing-place of the Normans it could also have been the embarkation-place of Dermot. There is on the north-western side of the present estuary at Bannow a little port named St Kerin's or St Kearn's, which was used by coasters as recently as the 1940s. Now the name of one of the rivers flowing into the Skar estuary at Bannow is the Corock and if we combine the two names we get *Corock-Kerin* which with some elision easily becomes *Corkeran.* I feel that this was Dermot's point of embarkation. It was within his own territory of Uí Ceinnsealaigh, and there was a port here, with fishing vessels and coasters at hand. Having embarked at this little port, Dermot would have been in a position to advise the Normans as to the suitability of Bannow Island as a beach-head.

Grattan Flood, *inter alia,* says *Auliffe O'Kinad* was probably a Danish retainer of MacMurrough named Olaf O'Kenny. The O'Kennys or Kennys were in this part of County Wexford in the twelfth century – and still are, for that matter
9 Edmund Curtis, *A History of Ireland*, chap. III, p. 46

6 The Normans

1 *Ireland under the Normans*, vol. I, chap. I
2 Curtis, *A History of Ireland*, vol. I, p. 47
3 *Ireland under the Normans*, vol. I, p. 80

4 *Expugnatio Hibernica*
5 Curtis, *A History of Ireland*, vol. I, p. 48
6 *The Geraldines*, part I, pp. 18-19
7 'When Dermot sought Wales he sought no unknown or foreign land,' writes Rev G. T. Stokes in *Ireland and the Anglo-Norman Church*, pp. 50-52 (London, 1889). 'He sought a country with which communication constant and helpful had been kept up for centuries, and specially for the previous century and a half. Dermot's forefathers and his Danish allies had been much more closely involved in the history of the Norman conquest of England and the tragic struggles of Edward the Confessor, of Harold, and of William the Conqueror than is usually believed. The kingdom of Leinster was always bounded by, and even at times embraced, the great Danish settlements of Dublin, Waterford, and Wexford. These places formed harbours of refuge where fugitive English rebels found safety and succour.'

Dr Stokes goes on to list the comings and goings between Wales and Ireland, mentioning a Welsh prince named Rhys who retreated into Ireland in 1087, the Irish fleets which were hired to intervene in Welsh quarrels, as in 1143, and the case of Gruffydd, son of Rhys ap Tewdwr, prince of south Wales, who crossed to Ireland about 1113 and lay concealed for years from the power of Henry I. Dermot MacMurrough's own great-grandfather (also named Dermot) had aided the Saxon King Harold and the other sons of Earl Godwin, later the opponents of William the Conqueror in 1051. The brothers crossed to Dublin where Dermot received them and furnished them with troops for an invasion of England. Sixteen years later, Harold's three sons repeated the process when driven out of England by the Norman invader. They also crossed to Dublin, where Dermot and the Norse provided them with a fleet of fifty-two ships with which they attacked Bristol (June 1069).

There were many intermarriages also between Irish, Welsh and Norman. In 1100 Gerald of Windsor was sent over to seek from Muirceartach O'Brien, 'King of Ireland', his daughter Lafracoth as a wife for Arnulf, lord of Pembroke, who was in revolt against Henry I and who sought an alliance with the Irish. Arnulf, though marrying Lafracoth and getting the aid he required, was later driven out of Wales, and spent some time in exile in Ireland. It may have been Alice, daughter of Arnulf and Lafracoth, who was later the wife of Maurice FitzGerald. Thus, it was to no strange country that Dermot MacMurrough set sail when he crossed to Wales in 1166. Indeed, it may have been these earlier Irish-Norman connections which provided the seed-bed for the idea of conquest in the minds of the Geraldines and Strongbow at the time of Dermot's visits

7 Laudabiliter

1 William Camden, *Britannia* (1610), section on Ireland, pp. 68-9
2 *Metalogicus* (for October 1159). Quoted in Webb's *John of Salisbury* (Methuen, 1932), p. 95
3 Largely compiled from the ancient *Book of Howth*, the original of which is believed to be in the Lambeth Library in London. Dr Meredith Hanmer, a prebendary of St Canice, wrote his *Chronicle* in 1571
4 The *Catholic Encyclopedia* (Caxton, London 1909), vol. V, pp. 118-121
5 I have yet to see it argued whether this 'Donation', in view of its dubious origin, could have been morally and legally used as a basis of *Laudabiliter's* terms
6 O'Doherty, 'Rome and the Anglo-Norman Invasion of Ireland', *The Irish Ecclesiastical Record*, vol. XLII, 1933
7 Ua Clerigh transcription of *Book of Leinster* text
8 Abbé James MacGeoghegan, a native of County West-meath, who lived for many years in France and who published his *History of Ireland* in Paris in 1758. This history was translated from the original French by Patrick O'Kelly and published in Dublin in 1835. It was republished in 1844 by Duffy of Dublin. The Abbé MacGeoghegan died in Paris in 1755
9 In *Cambrensis Eversus*
10 John Lanigan, a native of Cashel, was born in 1758. He studied at the Irish College in Rome, became a Doctor of Divinity and, in 1790, was appointed Professor of Ecclesiastical History, Scriptures and Hebrew at the University of Pavia. In 1796 he returned to Dublin and was appointed translator and editor of the works published by the Dublin Society. He was appointed the Society's librarian in 1808. He published his monumental four-volume *Ecclesiastical History of Ireland* in 1822. He died in 1828

11 'Rome and the Anglo-Norman Invasion of Ireland', *Irish Ecclesiastical Record*, vol. XLII, 1933
12 Curtis, *A History of Ireland*, chapter IV, p. 56
13 Last preface to *Expugnatio Hibernica*
14 *The Course of Irish History*, chapter VII, 'Ireland in the Eleventh and Twelfth Centuries', pp. 116-121
15 Ua Clerigh (*The History of Ireland*, vol. I, page 398) comments: 'The course he (Dermot) took after his flight was such as might have been reasonably expected. When an underlord or chieftain was unjustly attacked he appealed for succour or protection in the last resort to the High King or overlord. But if the true overlord of all was the Pope, and Henry was his vice-gerent (and there can be no doubt that this was the orthodox teaching at the time, of the regular if not of the secular clergy in the south of Ireland), if unable to stand alone against O'Connor and his allies, and if the Northern Uí Néill were not in a position to help him, to whom could Diarmuid appeal for succour and redress but to Henry, after his expulsion and flight?'

8 Recruiting

1 *MacCarthaigh's Book*
2 *MacCarthaigh's Book*
3 *Expugnatio Hibernica*
4 *The Song of Dermot and the Earl*
5 Strongbow was also earl of Striguil, the old Welsh name for Chepstow – it means 'the bend', and the River Wye makes a sharp bend as it passes the town of Chepstow
6 *Annals of the Four Masters* (Geraghty ed., 1846), pp. 10-11
7 *MacCarthaigh's Book*
8 This grant was later effected. Robert died before 1189 and Raymond le Gros succeeded to his inheritance
9 *Expugnatio Hibernica*. Author's note: From the tops of some of the hills in the St David area it is possible on clear days to make out mountains in south-east Ireland
10 *The Song of Dermot and the Earl*
11 *Ireland under the Normans*, vol. I, pp. 391-2
12 Herbert F. Hore, the Wexford historian, wrote in the *Journal of the Cambrian Archaeological Association*, New Series, No. X, in April 1852: 'Roche: A parish in the hundred of Rhos in Pembrokeshire gives its name to a family which was

distinguished and ennobled in Ireland. The name is derived from the rock on which Roche Tower so picturesquely stands, from whence the family were styled in ancient French deeds *de la Roche*, and in Latin *de Rupe*. They possessed extensive estates in Pembrokeshire . . . In the reign of Henry III Sir Gerald Roche possessed five Knights' fees of land in the County of Wexford.'

13 *Foras Feasa ar Eirinn*, book II, p. 326
14 Wright, *History of the Conquest of Ireland*, footnote, p. 189
15 *Annals of the Four Masters*, 1167

9 Preparation

1 Curtis, *A History of Ireland*, chapter IV, p. 49
2 *History of the Conquest of Ireland*, footnote, p. 188
3 The list is by no means exhaustive. It is merely illustrative of the places of origin of the first settlers
4 *Journal of the Waterford and South-East Ireland Archaeological Society*, vol. V, p. 232
5 Camden, *Britannia* (1610)

10 Invasion

1 I have myself, in a Kilmore Quay trawler, crossed St George's Channel to Milford Haven and back and can vouch for its tidal turbulence, even in calm summer weather
2 *Journal of the Waterford and South-East of Ireland Archaeological Society*, vol. V
3 O'Flaherty's *Ogygia* (chap. XCIV, 1685) records that, on 11 May, Dermot, then at Ferns, received a letter from FitzStephen announcing his arrival. Holinshed says 'the debarkation was effected on the 11th May'.

   George Henry Bassett, in his *Wexford Directory*, says the invaders spent ten days in making preparations, erecting temporary dwellings, the site of FitzStephen's house being still pointed out (1885). The exact location of this reputed site has since been lost
4 Both Keating (*Foras Feasa ar Eirinn*) and Joyce (*Irish Placenames*, p. 108) have given the Irish name *Cuan an Bhainbh* to Bannow. This has been mistranslated as 'the harbour of the sucking pig'. Dr O'Donovan states that Banbh is a name proper to one of the ancient Firbolgian

chieftains of Ireland. Banbh, he says, was one of five Fir-bolgian brothers who divided Ireland between them. Another of the brothers was Slainge, whence Slaney. Keating, incidentally, confused or telescoped the first landing at Bannow with the fourth landing which took place in 1170 at Baginbun. He says the first invaders 'landed in the harbour of the Banbh, on the coast of the County of Wexford, at a place called Beag-an-Bun'. As he gives the date of this landing as 1170 he is obviously mixing up the two landings

5 We must, I feel, seek the origin of the name Bannow in a context other than Irish. If we remember that the Normans called it *la Banne* and if we relate that to *Bec a Banne* (*bec* being French for beak or promontory) we get a very likely derivation of the name of nearby Baginbun (*Bec a Banne*, the promontory at or near Bannow). Orpen's *Banue* comes very close to the *Banewe* of Hervey's deed. There is, of course, a school of thought which holds that Bannow is derived from *Bun-abhann*, Irish for 'end of the rivers', which is an accurate description of the place – but very bad Irish. The rivers which meet in the estuary of the Skar are the Owenduff and the Corock

6 *Journal of the Kilkenny Archaeological Society*, 1849-51

7 Southwell manuscript. Bannow Island is sometimes referred to as the island of Slaid or Slade in old documents. This name may be derived from the district called Slade, on the eastern side of Hook peninsula, beyond Baginbun

8 J. C. Tuomey, in a paper contributed to the *Journal of the Kilkenny Archaeological Society* of 1849-51

9 Clare or Clare's Island (after Richard de Clare?) may have been a look-out post for the invaders. Animal and bird bones have been found in excavations there – traces of a Norman occupation? Tradition has it that FitzStephen burned his ships on the shore, so that there could be no return to Wales. It is said that the act is commemorated in the three burning vessels on the coat of arms of Wexford town

10 At the time of the invasion Bannow village was probably a small fishing hamlet huddled round a church, the beautiful ruins of which still stand overlooking Bannow Bay. This church was added to and embellished by the Normans, who made Bannow the first corporate town in Ireland. It returned two members to the Irish Parliament up to the Union (1800). Both Bannow and another Norman town,

Clonmines, further up the river which empties into Bannow Bay, declined when the estuary silted up

123 Bannow Abbey

11 P. H. Hore, *History of Duncannon Fort and the Southern Part of the Barony of Shelburne* (London, 1904), p. 429
12 'History and Topography of the Parish of Hook', vol. V, p. 242
13 Charlemagne's Cross, in the Pass of Roncevalles, became a shrine for penitents making the famous pilgrimage to Compostella in Spain. At the foot of the cross passing pilgrims deposited smaller wooden crosses. It is believed that this custom of laying wooden crosses at wayside shrines, prevalent later in Normandy and Flanders, was introduced to south Wexford by the Norman and Flemish settlers. The custom is still alive in the Kilmore area

11 Attack

1 For much of this information about Norse Wexford I am indebted to Dr George W. Hadden's learned article on 'The Origin and Development of Wexford Town' in the *Journal of the Old Wexford Society*, vol. I, 1968
2 *Expugnatio Hibernica*
3 *Journal of the Old Wexford Society*, vol. I, 1968
4 *Journal of the Old Wexford Society*, vol. I, 1968
5 *Journal of the Waterford and South-East of Ireland Archaeological Society*, vol. V

12 Counter-Moves

1 *Historical Portraits of Irish Chieftains and Anglo-Norman Knights* (Longman's, Green & Co., 1871) *Vide* Smith's ed of *Froissart*, vol. II, p. 78
2 *The History of Ireland to the Coming of Henry II*, vol. I, p. 402
3 *Ireland under the Normans*, vol. I, p. 160
4 *Historical Portraits of Irish Chieftains*, pp. 61-2
5 *Ireland under the Normans*, vol. I, p. 164
6 Holinshed, *Chronicles* (1577)
7 Maurice de Prendergast returned to Ireland shortly afterwards – probably with Strongbow in 1170. He took part in Strongbow's campaigns in the south before eventually joining the Order of the Knights of St John of Jerusalem. He became prior of the Order's house at Kilmainham and died there in 1205
8 Whence Duffry. Sections of this ancient fastness afforded shelter to Wexford fighters as late as 1798
9 MacGeoghegan, *History of Ireland*
10 *MacCarthaigh's Book*
11 Contrary to common belief, the castle which stands on the northern bank of the Slaney at Ferrycarrig is not Fitz-Stephen's original fortification. The latter, built of earth and wood, stood where the fake round tower now rises, on the southern side of the gorge

13 Baginbun

1 Dermot's father, Donncadh, who had been king of Dublin as well as of Leinster, was killed by the Norse in Dublin in 1115 and a dog buried with his body. (*See* chap. 4)
2 *Foras Feasa ar Eirinn*, p. 331
3 Translator of Giraldus's *Expugnatio Hibernica* (1587)
4 In a paper read to the Royal Society of Antiquaries of Ireland, 29 March 1898, and published in the Society's *Journal*, vol. XXVIII, p. 155 *et seq.*, in that same year
5 They may, indeed, be the remains of one of Fionn MacCumhail's residences. In the *Book of Lecan* there is a poem, attributed to Fionn, which refers to Druim Dean or the mansion on a hill. The story is told that Fionn, who was a Leinsterman, dwelt 'at Rinn a' Dubhain on the east side of the Barrow' (*Book of Leinster*, transcribed from an older manuscript). Rinn a'Dubhain is the old Irish name for the Hook peninsula, of which Baginbun forms part. On one

occasion Fionn was absent in Connacht and his residence at Druim Dean was destroyed by a chief named Uinche. Fionn, on his return, pursued and killed Uinche and then addressed a poem to the hill. It began:

Fornocht do dhinn, a Dhruim Dean
(Desolate is your mansion, O Druim Dean)

It is possible that the ancient earthworks and trenches, and the charred and burnt bones found on Baginbun Head, owe their origin to Fionn and the Fianna. The site, on the smaller headland jutting eastwards, has all the markings of a typical Celtic promontory fort

6 *Expugnatio Hibernica*, chapter XIII
7 *Foras Feasa ar Eirinn*, p. 333. As Raymond remained more than three months at Baginbun he had time to erect this 'strong embankment'. It is possible he first built the 'slight fortification' described by Giraldus
8 Programme, 'Excursion Round the Coast of Ireland'. Royal Society of Antiquaries of Ireland (1904)
9 *History of the Conquest of Ireland* (vol. I, p. 71) refers to 'Fitz-Stephen's Tent', a space like the foundations of a house in the middle of the camp area on the outer promontory; old Ordnance Survey maps mark the site as of 'Strongbow's Tent'. Tradition adds further confusion by referring to the Mine Holes under the promontory as 'Strongbow's Cave' and to the isolated rock at the point of the promontory as 'Cromail's (Cromwell's?) Rock'. The old Irish name is 'Maelogue'
10 Hooker, in a note to the 1587 edition of Giraldus's *Expugnatio Hibernica*, says that 'the Banna and the Boenne . . . were the names (as common fame is) of the two greatest ships in which the Englishmen there arrived.' Orpen makes this comment (*Ireland under the Normans*, vol. I, p. 183): 'Common fame derives this strange name from the two greatest ships in which the Englishmen there arrived. It used sometimes to be written "Bagg and Bunn", and *la Bague* and *la Bonne* are not improbable names of Norman ships.'

I, myself, doubt if the Normans who landed at Baginbun needed two ships at all. After all they were only about eighty in number and could have voyaged in one vessel. I have even greater doubt about this derivation of the name Baginbun. My own suggestion of *Bec a Banne* (the promontory at or near the Banne) still stands. The description admirably fits the place and would be just what Raymond and his men, their eyes on Bannow across the bay, might call this new landing-place

124 Promentory of Baginbun

11 *The Song of Dermot and the Earl*
12 'Raymond struck the first man of them who crossed the moat on the head with his sword, and split his head in two.' (*MacCarthaigh's Book*). In the original Irish the word used for moat is *diic*, which suggests that a trench had already been dug as part of the defences
13 A stratagem imitated successfully over six hundred years later at Enniscorthy when Father John Murphy forced the Duffry Gate by driving a herd of cattle ahead of his men in May 1798
14 Raymond later married Strongbow's sister Basilia and was appointed constable of Leinster. After Strongbow's death in June 1176, he was chief governor for a period. Although Giraldus says that Raymond had no legitimate children, nevertheless he has been claimed as the ancestor of the Graces, the FitzMaurices (barons of Lixnaw) and the Redmonds of the Hall (now Loftus Hall), Hook peninsula
15 In his 'Description of Ireland', published with Holinshed's *Chronicles* in 1577; the earliest quotation in print of this 'old ancient rhyme' about the battle at Baginbun. A plaque, built into a miniature Norman keep, was unveiled at Baginbun on 17 May 1970, in commemoration of Raymond's landing there. It was removed overnight and has not been replaced

14 Strongbow

1 Some historians hold that the wedding took place in Reginald's Tower but there is no authority for this. Orpen

says that in all probability the ceremony took place in the Christ Church of the Holy Trinity some days after the taking of the town. In any case Reginald's Tower would have been far too small for what was undoubtedly a huge congregation

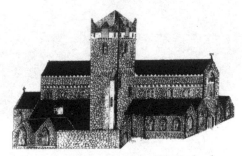

125 *Christ Church, Waterford*

2 *Annals of the Four Masters*, 1170
3 T. Leland, *History of Ireland* (London, 1773)
4 But see also footnote 2, chap. 4
5 A footnote in the Bryan Geraghty edition of the *Annals of the Four Masters* (1846) says that the disease afflicting Dermot 'is supposed to have been the *morbus pedicularis* of medical writers'. This is an infestation of lice, though not usually fatal. Lice, however, are concerned in the transmission of typhus, trench fever, etc., to any one of which Dermot could have been subjected. Another suggestion is that Dermot suffered from venereal disease. My own opinion is that he may have died from leprosy, contracted from some of the Normans who had been on the Crusades in the Holy Land. *Cf.* William Ferrand, the leper who fought so desperately at Baginbun

15 Siege

1 *Expugnatio Hibernica*, chap. XVII. The practice of selling their children as slaves to the Irish and the Norse of Ireland was common among the Anglo-Saxon people, according to Giraldus. Bristol was the chief centre of this trade
2 I have followed here the sequence of events as given by Giraldus in *Expugnatio Hibernica*. The *Annals of Tighernach* also give this sequence, in which the Norse assault occurs first, in June. This is followed by the siege of Dublin by

Ruairi and his great army, which is finally broken in September. Curtis (*A History of Medieval Ireland,* 1923), A. J. Otway Ruthven (*A History of Medieval Ireland,* 1968), and Rev F. X. Martin (*The Course of Irish History,* chap. VIII) concur.

Another version of the events is found in *The Song of Dermot* which has Ruairi besieging Dublin first, his army being beaten by a Norman assault, and then the arrival of Asculf and his fleet of Norse ships and the attack on the east gate. Orpen (*Ireland under the Normans,* vol. I) follows this line of thought. Either way the outcome was identical. The Normans held on to Dublin which, for the next seven hundred and fifty years, was to be the seat of English power in Ireland

3   The 60,000 figure must be doubted. Half this number might be nearer the mark

4   *The Song of Dermot*

5   *The Song of Dermot*

6   *Expugnatio Hibernica*

7   Hanmer, in *Chronicle,* p. 261

8   According to the *Annals of the Four Masters* a further attempt to take Dublin was made later (in September 1171) by that doughty old warrior O'Rourke of Breifne, but it failed. The *Annals of the Four Masters* also give this version of the defeat of the Irish at Castleknock: 'Roderick O'Connor, Tiernan O'Rourke and Murchadh O'Carroll marched with an army to Dublin to besiege the city, then in the possession of Earl Strongbow and Miles de Cogan. They remained there for a fortnight, during which time many fierce engagements took place. The king marched through Leinster with the cavalry of Breifne and Oriel and burned the corn of the English. While Roderick was thus engaged Earl Strongbow and Miles de Cogan attacked the camp of the northern Irish, slew many soldiers and captured their provisions, armour and horses.' As propaganda for Ruairi this may be useful; as history it is not very reliable

9   The entry in the *Annals of the Four Masters* recording Ruairi's death runs as follows: 'Roderick O'Connor, king of Connacht and of all Ireland, both English and Irish, died in canonical orders at Cong, after sincere repentance, victorious over the world and the devil: his body was conveyed to Clonmacnoise and was interred there, on the north side of the altar of the great church.' Ruairi, 82 at the

time of his death, had abdicated his throne in 1184 after a reign of eighteen years. He was in seclusion at Cong for thirteen years. He was interred in the same tomb as his father, High-King Turlough O'Connor, in the cathedral of St Ciaran at Clonmacnoise

16 Henry

1 Meiler FitzHenry, grandson of King Henry I and natural son of Henry FitzHenry, was chief justice of Ireland from 1199 to 1209. He founded the abbey of Great Connell in County Kildare and was buried there in 1220

2 The English historian Sir James Ware (1594-1666) says he saw a copy of the confirmation charter of this grant, given by King John to William Marshall, earl of Pembroke who married Strongbow's daughter and heiress Isabel. (*Works of Sir James Ware Concerning Ireland*, Dublin, 1739)

3 It is also worthy of note that Henry's army consisted largely of English soldiers, an indication, perhaps, of his mistrust of Normans and Flemings

4 MacGeoghegan, *A History of Ireland*

5 Holinshed, *Chronicles*: 'He subtly alleged that he submitted Connacht but not the command of all Ireland.'

6 Stokes, *Ireland and the Anglo-Norman Church* (London, 1889), says this Norse conference site was on top of the hill where St Andrew's Church now stands in Andrew's Street, off Dame Street, Dublin

7 See chap. 7

8 Though Henry was anxious to be reconciled with the pope, he did not do public penance for the murder of Becket (now St Thomas, as he had been canonised since his murder in 1170) until 1173. Charles Knight records the scene: 'On the 10th of July, Henry rode from Southampton during the night, and as he saw the cathedral towers of Canterbury looming in the grey dawn, he alighted, and walked in penitential garb barefoot to the city. He knelt at the tomb of Becket in deep humiliation. The bishop of London preached … then the great king, before the assembled monks and chapter, poured fourth his contrition for the passionate exclamation which had been so rashly interpreted, and he was scourged with a knotted cord. He spent the night in the dark crypt and next day rode fasting to London.' Charles Knight, *History of England*, vol. 1, p. 301

17 Aftermath

1 *Expugnatio Hibernica*
2 *Miscellaneous Annals*, p. 71: Curtis, *A History of Medieval Ireland*, p. 83, says FitzStephen died in 1185. This would have permitted Giraldus to visit him in 1183
3 According to the Carew Manuscript (in Lambeth) Raymond was buried in the abbey of Molana, or Dairinnis, near Youghal
4 What is commonly known as 'Strongbow's Tomb' in Christ Church, a monument showing the effigy of a knight in armour, is not in fact the earl's tombstone.

Laurence O'Toole himself died four years later. He had incurred the enmity of Henry II through his efforts to rally the Irish against the invaders. In 1180 he went to England to see Henry who treated him in far from courteous manner and prevented his return to Ireland. Henry then went to France and Laurence followed him with a view to conciliation. But in Normandy he was struck down by fever of which he soon afterwards died, on 14 November 1180, in the monastery of Eu. He was interred in the church of the monastery and was canonised by Pope Honorius III in 1226
5 After Strongbow died, Chepstow Castle was held again by Henry II, this time as ward for Isabel, Strongbow's

*126 Henry II
at Canterbury*

unmarried daughter and heir. She lived in the castle protected by a royal constable, a chaplain and his clerk, a porter, three watchmen, ten men-at-arms, ten archers, and a further fifteen men-at-arms for whom the castle was their base camp. She married William Marshall in 1189. She had five sons, two of whom were to die violently and all of whom died childless. She also had five daughters who inherited her estates. Alan Reid, *The Castles of Wales* (London, 1973), pp. 58-9

6 De Lacy was killed at Durrow in County Laois. Cambrensis chronicles the event: 'On a time, as each man was busily occupied – some lading, some heaving, some planting, some growing, the general himself also digging with a pickage; a desperate villaine among them, whose tools the nobleman was using, espieing both his hands occupied and his bodie inclining downwards still as he stroke, watched as he so stopped, and with an axe cleft his head in sunder, little esteeming the torments that for this traiterous act ensued. His bodie was buried at Bective and his head in St Thomas Abbei at Dublin'

7 Among those who came in John's household party was his chaplain, our chronicler Giraldus Cambrensis

Epilogue

1 *The Course of Irish History*, chapter VIII, 'The Anglo-Norman Invasion', pp. 137 *et seq*

2 Dr John O'Donovan, in a note in his edition of the *Annals of the Four Masters* says: 'The editor, when examining the baronies of Forth and Bargie for the Ordnance Survey, was particularly struck with the difference between the personal appearance of the inhabitants of these baronies and those of O'Murphy's country, the northern baronies of the County Wexford. The Kavanaghs and Murphys are tall and often meagre, while the Flemings, Codds, and other natives of the baronies of Forth and Bargie are generally short and stout.' As we have seen, most of the chief men of the invasion were stout, short or of middle height rather than tall. Raymond le Gros – 'very stout and a little above middle height'; Meiler FitzHenry – 'below the middle height, broad chested'; Raymond FitzHugh – 'short in stature,' etc. The present-day stature of Wexfordmen, as exemplified in the famous county hurling teams of the 1950s, may be said to be a blend of Gaelic height and Norman girth.

The peculiar *Yola* dialect which was spoken in Forth and Bargy until the nineteenth century owed its origin to the early colonists

3 *The Lament for John MacWalter Walsh, with Notes on the History of the Family of Walsh from 1170 to 1690* (Kelmscott Press, New York, 1925), pp. 46-7
4 *The Course of Irish History*, chapter VIII, p. 139
5 *Ireland under the Normans*, preface vol. I
6 *The Course of Irish History*, chapter VIII, pp. 142-3

127 Tomb of Geoffrey de Marisco

Notes on Illustrations and Sources

Cover: Seal of Richard de Clare, earl of Pembroke, surnamed 'Strongbow'. 'There is a pleasure, which seems almost universal, afforded by seeing and handling some relique which has been seen and handled by men who were remarkable in their times ... I envy not the man who can look on this charter and see nought but a shred of discoloured parchment and a morsel of crumbling wax – whose mind does not the more vividly form to itself a picture of the time when the Cambro-Norman husband of MacMurrough's daughter parcelled out her regal inheritance amongst those hardy and warlike followers whose good lances and trenchant blades were his best title-deeds to the kingdom of Leinster.' (Rev James Graves, from notes to an exhibition in Ormond Castle, Co Kilkenny in 1851)

1. Jerpoint Abbey, Co Kilkenny, was founded in 1180 for the Cistercians as a daughter house of Baltinglass, Mellifont and Clairvaux. It was one of the wealthiest monastic foundations, with demense lands of over 1,500 acres. At the dissolution of the monasteries the buildings and lands were granted to Thomas Butler, tenth earl of Ormond, at an annual rent of £49.3s.9d. The tomb slab of the two Norman knights is exceptionally fine. (Office of Public Works)

2. The stone figure from Jerpoint Abbey holds a shield which resembles that of the le Poer (Power) family. (Office of Public Works)

3. The typical motte-and-bailey (mound and courtyard) castle of the Normans consisted of a large mound, on the summit of which was erected a keep of timber (later of stone). The courtyard or bailey on the lower level had residential buildings, kitchens, workshops and stables. (Drawing Terry Myler)

4. Reconstruction of a Norman ship. Length could be from 80 to 140 feet, with a breadth of 16 to 28 feet, pulled by 16 to 30 oars a side. There was a single square sail, surmounted by a signal lantern and it was steered by a rudder. The platforms at either end date from a later century. (Drawing Terry Myler)

5. Manorbier Castle in Pembrokeshire, Wales, was the birthplace, in 1146, of Gerald de Barri, Gerald of Wales (Giraldus Cambrensis). He described it as 'excellently well defended by turrets and bulwarks ... having on the northern and southern sides a fine fish-pond under its walls, as conspicuous for its grand appearance as for the depth of its waters.' The first castle dates from the beginning of the twelfth century, with many additions during the following century. (Cadw: Welsh Historic Monuments. Crown Copyright)

6. Page from the vellum volume, executed c.1200, which contains the two works of Giraldus Cambrensis concerning Ireland – *Topographia Hiberniae* and *Expugnatio Hibernica*. There are many marginal illustrations; the significance of this one is explained in the note for p. 15. (Ms 700: National Library of Ireland)

7. Another page from *Topographia*; the illustration relates to a story about two men west of the Shannon who told a traveller that they had never heard of Christ and Christianity and were similarly ignorant of weeks, months and years. (Ms 700: National Library of Ireland)

8. Map of Europe from the Giraldus Ms. Ireland (at the bottom of the map) shows the areas of Norman influence – Dublin, Wexford, Waterford and Limerick, the rivers Shannon, Suir, Slaney and Liffey. England, similarly, lists the Norman towns – London, Lincoln, York and Winchester. On the European mainland, Norway is to the left, Spain to the right, with France and Italy in the centre. The map probably served as a guide for travel from England to Rome, via Paris, Lyon, the Alps, Pavia, and Piacenza. (Ms 700: National Library of Ireland)

9. First page of *Le Chansun de Dermot e li Quens Ricard FizGilbert* – The Song of Dermot and the Earl. (Ms 596: Lambeth Palace Library)

10. Irish scribe. (Ms 700: National Library of Ireland)

11. Ptolemy's map of Ireland c.150 AD. Names are given in English where identification is reasonably certain. Capital

letters indicate tribes, lower case indicates towns. (Terry Myler, from reconstruction by F. J. Byrne)

12 Wexford county and surrounding countryside. (Terry Myler)

13 Cormac's Chapel, Cashel, Co Tipperary was built by Cormac MacCarthy, king of Munster. The annals record the consecration, with great ceremony, of the stone-roofed chapel in 1134. It is both the largest and best example of Irish Romanesque art in Ireland. (W. H. Bartlett, *The Scenery and Antiquities of Ireland*, London, vol. 1, p. 141)

14 West doorway of Clonfert Cathedral, Co Galway, which dates from the twelfth century. The Irish Romanesque doorway has six receding planes, decorated with heads, leaves and abstract patterns. Within the triangular pediment are five arcades which are sculpted with heads and there are more heads in the recesses leading to the apex. (Irish Tourist Board)

15 Mairead Dunlevy in *Dress in Ireland* writes: 'The reputed inauguration ceremony of the Cenél Conaill. The king-elect slaughtering the white mare (a symbol of the territorial goddess) is shown wearing a dark green *fallaing* over off-white trews. When bathing in the mare's blood he is surrounded by men wearing fawn, dark green and yellow tunics. All men wear a version of the *culan* hairstyle in which the front of the head was shaved and the hair left long at the back.' (Ms 700: National Library of Ireland)

16 Irish dress – a loose outer tunic, with baggy trews caught in at the ankles. (Terry Myler)

17 Francis Grose describes this illustration as 'an Irishman in the dress of 1185, as described by Giraldus Cambrensis. He is armed with two darts and a lance, has the conical cap, over his shoulders the *cappuce*, under that the *fallin* or jacket, and then braccae or breeches and stockings of one piece.' (Francis Grose, *The Antiquities of Ireland*, Dublin, 1791, vol. 1, facing p. xxiii)

18-19-20-21-22. Occupations for the months of the year, from a calendar prefixed to a Hymnarium of the eleventh century. The months illustrated are May – watching sheep (18); March – breaking up soil, digging and sowing (19); July – haymaking (20); September – pasturing swine (21); December – threshing and winnowing (22). (John Richard Green, *A Short History of the English People*, London, 1892, vol. 1, pp. 155-8)

23. The *Breac Maedhóig*, the shrine of St Aidan, first bishop of Ferns, who died on 31 January 632. The shrine, which dates from the eleventh or twelfth century, is of bronze with gilt bronze panels and has amber and glass studs around the base. A. T. Lucas described the figures as 'the most powerful and realistic representations of the human figure in Irish art'. The saint's relics are enshrined in the casket, which, together with its leather satchel, can be seen in the National Museum. (National Museum of Ireland)

24. Map of Ireland, showing the main kingdoms before the Norman invasion and the clans who held the territory. The Norse settlements around Dublin, Wexford, Waterford, Cork and Limerick are shaded. (Terry Myler)

25. Map of Waterford city as it may have looked about 1050. The line of the complete wall of 1050 is shown, also the portion still existing in 1989. (Terry Myler, after the map in *Reginald's Tower and the Story of Waterford* by Patrick Mackey, Waterford, 1980)

26. The grianan of Aileach, the seat of the kings of the northern Uí Néill, at Carrowreagh on the Inishowen peninsula in Co Donegal, was occupied from the fifth until the twelfth century. It is an earthen hill fort with three outer rings of defence within which stands a circular stone fort with wall walks. It was extensively reconstructed in the last century. (Aerial photography by Daphne Pochin Mould)

27. Dermot MacMurrough. He wears a fawn-yellow tunic with loose sleeves, a white belt, green trews and black shoes. (Ms 700: National Library of Ireland)

28. This vellum deed, the earliest in the National Library collection, confirms a grant of lands made by Dermot's liegeman Dermot Ua Riáin, king of Idrone (mainly in Co Carlow), to the Cistercian Jerpoint Abbey in Co Kilkenny. The lands were intended to endow a daughter house in Ua Riáin's territory near Goresbridge. Among the witnesses to the confirmation were Dermot's brother, his illegitimate son, and his cousin, Lorcan O'Toole, archbishop of Dublin. No trace of the abbey now remains. (Deed 1, Ormond Papers: National Library of Ireland)

29. Baltinglass Abbey, Co Wicklow, was founded by the Cistercians in 1148 as a daughter house of Mellifont. According to Grose, the bishop was mitred and sat in parliament. (F. Grose, *Antiquities,* vol. 2, between pp. 6 and 7)

30. Edward Ledwich gives this account of St Patrick's Purgatory: 'The very year after the Council of Kells, AD 115, Matt. Paris relates the visions of Owen, an Irish soldier, which he saw in St Patrick's Purgatory. The story was taken up by Henry, a Cistercian monk, and varnished with all the powers of his ingenuity. Christ, says he, appeared to St. Patrick, and leading him to a desert place showed him a deep hole, and told him, whoever repented and was armed with true faith, and entering that pit continued there a night and a day, should be purged from all his sins; and also, during his abode there, should not only see the pains of the damned, but the joys of the blessed. St Patrick immediately built a church on the spot and placed therein regular canons of St Austin.

'This impious fiction, for many ages firmly believed, confutes itself by mentioning regular canons, which were well known to have had no existence before the 10th century. The groundwork of this story and many of the particulars are taken from Bede, and so is the name, Owen ... it has been well remarked that no account of this purgatory is to be found in any writer previous to the 12th century.

'This purgatory is in a small isle in Lough Derg, in the southern part of Donegal. The isle is but 126 yards long by 44 broad, and the cave is fifteen feet and a half by two wide, and so low that a tall man cannot stand erect in it without great inconvenience. The floor is the natural rock, and the whole is covered with large stones and sods. There are seven chapels and circles dedicated to St Patrick, St Abage, St Molass, St Brendan, St Columba, St Catherine and St Bridget.'

The purgatory was demonished by order of Pope Alexander VI in 1497 but Ledwich notes that 'the place is still frequented in the months of May, June and July.' (Edward Ledwich, *Antiquities of Ireland*, Dublin, 1790, p. 447)

31. With magnificently and elaborately carved Romanesque doorways, the Nuns' Church at Clonmacnoise, Co Offaly, stands some way upstream from the main monastic foundation. Clonmacnoise was, after Armagh, the greatest of the early monastic schools. The group of buildings on the left part of the Shannon has nine churches, two twelfth-century round towers, five high crosses, and more

than five hundred carved gravestones. (Office of Public Works)

32. Mellifont, the first Cistercian abbey in Ireland, was founded in 1142 by St. Malachy, who brought in monks from St Bernard's Abbey at Clairvaux in France. The octagonal lavabo dates from *c*.1200. (F. Grose, *Antiquities,* vol. 2, p. 6)

33–34. The page from the *Book of Leinster* on which was written the news of Dermot's departure from Ireland. The page of the facsimile was treated chemcially at one time which has resulted in a clouding of the lettering.

The *Book of Leinster,* the earliest manuscript wholly in Irish was written over a period of years in the mid-twelfth century by six scribes, one of whom was Aed MacCrimthainn, tutor to Dermot MacMurrough. Largely historical, this monumental work includes the *Lebor Gabála*, an account of pre-historic invasions; the 'War of the Gael with the Gaill', which deals with the Norman invasion of Ireland; lists of the rulers of Ireland and its provinces and kingdoms; a version of the cattle-raid of Cooley; and miscellaneous texts, genealogies, anecdotes and versified history. Acquired by Trinity College, Dublin, in 1786 as part of the Sir John Sebright collection, *Treasures of the Library* describes it as a 'summation of the native learning of Ireland down to the twelfth century ... history as understood by the men of the twelfth century'. (Ms 1339, fol. 200r, facs. p. 275; reproduced by permission of the Board of Trinity College Dublin)

35. Cilgerran Castle, Pembrokeshire. One of the marcher lordships established by Henry I in Wales, Cilgerran was held by Gerald de Windsor, husband of Nesta. It changed hands several times over the next centuries before being recaptured, in 1223, by the eldest son of William Marshall and Isabel, Strongbow's daughter. (Cadw: Welsh Historic Monuments; Crown Copyright)

36. Map of Europe showing the Norman expansion from Normandy – north to England and Ireland, south-west to Brittany, Anjou, Touraine, Poitou, Aquitaine and Gascony, south-east to Naples, Sicily, Malta, Crete and the Holy Land. (Terry Myler)

37. The reverse of the second great seal of William the Conqueror. J.R. Green considers that this is 'the best authentic portrait of the first Norman king of England.' (*A*

Short History of the English People, p. 151)
38. Reverse of the fourth seal of Henry I. The words *Henricus Dei gratia dux Normannorum* shows that it dates from after 1066. (*A Short History of the English People,* p. 169)
39. Maurice FitzGerald. (Ms 700: National Library of Ireland).
40. A Welsh archer from an entry-book of Edward I's time, formerly among the documents pertaining to the Treasury of Receipt of Exchequer, and kept in the chapter-house at Westminster. Now in the British Public Record Office. (*A Short History of the English People,* p. 315)
41. The seal of Empress Matilda, mother of Henry II. The wording *Mathildis Romanorum Regina* shows it was made for her in Germany before her first husband's crowning in Rome in AD 1111. (*A Short History of the English People,* p. 194)
42. Great seal of Henry II. (Charles Knight, *The Popular History of England,* London, 1862, p. 270)
43–44. St Thomas excommunicating his enemies (left), and arguing with Henry II and Louis VII of France (43); parting of St Thomas and the two kings (44). (From *Vie de St Thomas,* a French life of the saint written in England 1230–1260. Reproduced from facsimiles in an edition published by Society des Anciens Textes Francais: (*A Short History of the English People,* p. 205)
45. Assassination of St Thomas of Cantenbury. (Drawn by Matthew Paris in the margin of his Greater Chronicle: Ms Corpus Christi College, Cambridge, XXVI. (*A Short History of the English People,* p. 207
46. Charles Knight writes: 'The Cistercians were established in England late in the reign of Henry I (1100–1135). Their rule was one of severe mortification and of the strictest discipline. Their lives were spent in labour and in prayer and their one frugal daily meal was eaten in silence. Whilst other religious orders had their splendid abbeys amidst large communities, the Cistercians humbly asked grants of land in the most solitary places, where the recluse could meditate without interruption by his fellow-men, amidst desolate moors and in the uncultivated gorges of inaccessible mountains.' (*The Popular History of England,* p. 256)
47. Seal of St Anselm. William Rufus (1087–1100) left church positions vacant so as to enjoy the revenues which then reverted to the Crown. But during a serious illness in 1093

he sent for the then abbot of Bec and made him archbishop of Canterbury, an appointment he was to regret as Anselm defended Church interests which had been eroded by the Norman conquest. (*A Short History of the English People*, p. 167)

48. Excavations at Mellifont have exposed the foundations of a twelfth-century church and cloister, and of later thirteenth, fourteenth and fifteenth-century buildings. (Irish Tourist Board)

49. The dominions of the Angevin kings. The dotted line shows Dermot MacMurrough's journey to Poitiers in France in 1167, where he met Henry II; the solid line is the journey of Henry II to Ireland in 1171. (Terry Myler)

50. Henry II. (Ms 700: National Library of Ireland)

51. Chepstow (Striguil) Castle, in Monmouthshire, offers a good illustration of the feudal system at work. Probably begun in 1067 by William FitzOsbern, second cousin of William the Conqueror who made him an earl, his son lost both castle and title as a result of an attempted rebellion. Henry I granted the castle to Walter FitzRichard of the Clare family, as part of a massive grant of land covering Monmouthshire and Gloucestershire. He died without heir and the castle passed to his nephew, the first 'Strongbow', who was succeeded by Richard de Clare (the Irish 'Strongbow'). Henry II confiscated Strongbow's estates, including Chepstow, in 1170, but Strongbow regained possession in 1173. On his death the castle again reverted to the Crown and was held in trust for his daughter Isabel, whose sons enlarged it considerably. The keep is the most ancient part of the castle. (Cadw: Welsh Historic Monuments. Crown Copyright)

52. Robert FitzStephen. (Ms 700: National Library of Ireland)

53. Roch Castle, Pembrokeshire. The castle has been extensively restored but the tower on the rock is still a local landmark. Traces of the old earthwork bailey can be seen at the foot of the outcrop

54. The Norman knight on horseback was dressed in a hauberk or coat of mail. Though the Bayeux Tapestry seems to show that these hauberks ended in trouser legs, Sir James Mann in *The Bayeux Tapestry* (Phaidon Press) dismisses the idea and says that the skirts are divided back and front, as it would be impossible to ride in mail trousers without great discomfort to the fork. The banding

at wrist and legs was cloth, probably to soften the roughness. The helmet was a conical crown, with a broad flat nasal to protect the nose. The lance was light enough to be used as a javelin. Sometimes to denote authority it would have a gonfanon, a small rectangular banner with 'tails', attached. The shield, worn on the left side when on horseback, had a round top and a narrow pointed end.

The Welsh archers were usually dressed in tunics and breeches, though sometimes they wore coats of mail. The bow was not the long-bow of the later Middle Ages and was not drawn to the ear but only to the body. The quiver of arrows hung either from a shoulder-strap or a waist-band. Though these arrows could kill a man in chain-mail at fifty yards, they were ineffective against wood and leather shields. (Terry Myler, based on the Bayeux Tapestry)

55. Irish fighters, as depicted by Giraldus, seem woefully badly equipped when compared with the Normans. They had no armour or defensive gear and their baggy clothes are in sharp contrast to the streamlined Normans. Their favourite weapon was the axe, which would not, however, have been so scientifically designed as those of the Normans, which had curved heads to make a downward thrust more lethal. On horseback, they used neither saddle nor spurs. (Terry Myler, after *Topographia*)

56. The family tree of Nesta, daughter of Rhys ap Tewdwr, prince of south Wales, showing her descendants by her three marriages or liasions. The names in capital letters denote those who took part in the Norman invasion. (Terry Myler)

57. Norman crusaders, *c.*1100, wearing a slightly looser kind of hauberk than shown in the Bayeux Tapestry. Their swords, similar to those of Viking origin, had a broad blade honed to a fine edge. (H.W. Koch, *Medieval Warfare*, London, 1982: Mary Evans Picture Library)

58–59. Carrying arms and armour to the ships. The fact that two men carried the hauberks suggests they were heavy, but Sir Charles Gibbs-Smith (*The Bayeux Tapestry*) thinks they would not have weighed more than 20–25 lb (a fully armed Norman soldier carried about 45–50 lb compared to the 55 lb or so carried by the modern soldier).

Evidently an important item was the huge hogshead of wine being pulled along on a cart, which also carried helmets and lances. (Terry Myler, based on the Bayeux Tapestry)

60–61. The leaders arrive to embark, men and horses go abroad and the three ships sail. In the Bayeux Tapestry the shields are shown *inside* the gunwale – they would have been stored away before sailing in case the soldiers had to man the oars. The shields at bow and stern were anti-ramming devices. (Terry Myler, based on the Bayeux Tapestry)

62–63. The map of Wales and Wexford shows the route the three ships led by Robert FitzStephen would have travelled on their way to Bannow. An inset shows Bannow Bay. (Terry Myler)

63–64. Seamen unship the mast while horses are led ashore. The other two ships have arrived, and foraging for provisions, the invaders capture an ox, a sheep and a pig. (Terry Myler, based on the Bayeux Tapestry)

65   Map of Bannow area (Terry Myler)

66. William FitzAudelin and Meiler FitzHenry. FitzAudelin was to be one of few first-wave invaders that Henry II continued to trust. When Strongbow and de Lacy were summoned for military service by Henry in 1173. FitzAudelin was put in charge. FitzHenry was one of the four leading Normans who died childless because, claims Giraldus, 'of the violation of the sanctuary lands at Lismore'. (Ms 700: National Library of Ireland)

67–68–69–70. The Norman cavalry line up and gallop into battle, supported by archers on foot. An astute observer will note that in illustration 67 there are ten men on eight horses – that between them have only twenty-five legs. The charging knights have their lances held in upright, in horizontal, and in raised position ready to be hurled. (From *The Bayeux Tapestry*, ed. Sir Frank Stenton, Phaidon Press Ltd, London, 1956; photographs Percy Hennell)

71   Norse Wexford, with arrows indicating the Norman attack. (Terry Myler, after map by V. Staples)

72–73. The feast being prepared. Meat is boiled over a pot, bread is placed on a trencher, and spits of roasted meat are handed out. The food is placed on a rough sideboard and the principal guests are summoned by horn. The meal commences as servants hand up dishes. (*The Bayeux Tapestry*, Phaidon Press)

74. Francis Grose made this drawing of a rath, with the

comment: 'We have here the figure of our raths, being either natural or artificial conical hills, on which the natives had their habitations, and to which they resorted for security. They are seldom seen without one or more entrenchments.' (F. Grose, *Antiquities*, vol. 1, plate 40)

75. The group is rather similar to that in the abbey of Knockmoy – the figure in the centre was supposed to represent Ruairi O'Connor. (Irish Tourist Board)

76. Raymond le Gros. Though Giraldus described him as 'very stout', the illustration shows him, while not as willowy as Hervey, of average girth. (Ms 700: National Library of Ireland)

77. Map of the Baginbun area, showing the Celtic promontory fort and the Norman earthworks. (Terry Myler)

78. Baginbun, the beach and the cliffs. (Photograph: Flynn's Photo Service)

79–80. An officer (holding the gonfanon which signifies rank) gives orders for the erection of fortifications. The workmen are carrying metal-tipped spades which have only one foot-thread, and one has a splayed shovel. In 80, still supervised by an official, they are building a 'mound-castle' (motte) by throwing up soil; one has a curved pick. A wooden fortress is erected on top. (*The Bayeux Tapestry*, Phaidon Press)

81–82. The battle over, the victorious Normans ride in pursuit of the beaten enemy (*The Bayeux Tapestry*, Phaidon Press)

83. Hervey de Monte Marisco. He wears a long yellow tunic, with green hose and black shoes. His scabbard hangs from a white waist-band. (Ms 700: National Library of Ireland)

84. The tomb of Raymond le Gros, Molana Abbey, Co Waterford, sketched by Daniel Grose (1766–1838), a nephew of Francis Grose. Hardly an accurate portrayal as Raymond died before 1200 and the style of the carving, according to Roger Stalley, suggests a date of about 1300–50. The present whereabouts of the effigy are unknown. (Terry Myler, after Grose, *The Antiquities of Ireland, A Supplement to Francis Grose*, ed. Roger Stalley, Dublin, 1991, p. 11)

85–86. The first assault party under Robert FitzStephen embarked in three ships, which were probably already available. Strongbow's army, 'to the number of a thousand', would probably have needed new ships. The Normans were adept at building ships as the Bayeux

Tapestry shows. Here men are cutting down trees and planing planks. The shipbuilders are using adzes, small axes and drills for boring the oar-ports. The ships completed, they are dragged down to the shore, using ropes attached to a post. (Terry Myler, based on the Bayeux Tapestry)

87. Reginald's Tower, Waterford, was build in 1003 by Ragnvald, son of Sigtrygg, the Norseman who is generally credited with the founding of Viking Waterford, calling it *Vadre-fjord* or *Vedra-fjord*. It was situated on the easternmost angle of the city walls, near the river Suir. F. Grose, *Antiquities*, vol. I, unpaged)

88. Strongbow. (Ms 700: National Library of Ireland)

89. Fresco painting in Knockmoy Abbey, Co Galway, founded in 1189 by Cathal O'Connor. According to Ledwich, Cathal 'at the head of twenty thousand men', victorious over a Norman force after 'a most bloody and obstinate engagement', vowed to erect an abbey on the spot. The place was called in Irish, Knockmoy, the hill of the plain, and the abbey *Monasterium de colle victoriae*, from Cathal's success.

The fresco painting on the tomb of Cathal dates from a much later period, but clearly refers to the killing of Dermot MacMurrough's son. The figures on the top represent six kings, three deceased and three living. The centre figure is Ruairi O'Connor, high-king of Ireland: 'He holds in his hand the leaf of some plant, to denote his being Lord Proprietor of the whole Kingdom, the princes on each side are his vassals. He with the hawk on his fist is his grand Falconer, the other with the sword, his grand Marshall, these held their lands by grand Serjeanty. Below them sits a Brehon with his roll of Laws, having pronounced sentence of death on Dermod MacMurrough's son for the crime of his father, in joining the English. The boy is tied to a tree, and two Archers are executing the sentence, his body being transfixed with arrows. Such, I apprehend, is the story which this painting exhibits.' (Ledwich, *Antiquities*, between pp. 280 and 281)

90. Ferns Castle was built by the Normans about 1176, probably on the site of Dermot MacMurrough's 'stone house'. (F. Grose, *Antiquities*, vol. II, facing p. 77)

91. Charter from Strongbow, *c*.1172. (From the Ormond Papers, originally in Kilkenny Castle, now in the National

Library of Ireland)
92. Cambro-Norman knight and foot-soldier from the seal of Strongbow, Richard de Clare, earl of Pembroke. (Terry Myler, based on a nineteenth-century drawing in *The Oxford Illustrated History of Ireland*, ed. R. F. Foster, Oxford, 1989, p. 56)
93. Map of Dublin and neighbourhood, showing the Norse attack on the city, and the route of the Norman retreat from the city and their attack on Ruairi's camp at Castleknock. (Terry Myler)
94. The Augustinian abbey of Cong, Co Mayo was founded in the twelfth century by High-King Turlough O'Connor on the site of a seventh-century foundation of St. Fechin. Here Ruairi O'Connor died in 1198. The ruins of the church, cloister and chapter-house, which has some very fine windows and decorated stone work, still stand. (Office of Public Works)
95. A round tower and one of the richly carved high crosses at Clonmacnoise. Ruairi O'Connor is buried here, in the cathedral of St Ciaran, in the same tomb as his father, High-King Turlough. (Bartlett, *Scenery and Antiquities*, vol. 1, facing p. 104)
96. The first castle at Pembroke in Wales, erected in 1097 by Arnulph de Montgomery, was described as 'a slender fortress with stakes and turf'. Though the enormous round keep in the inner bailey at the north end of the site was not built until the end of the twelfth century, the illustration gives some idea of the strategic position of the castle. (*A Short History of the English People*, vol. 1, p. 314)
97. This illustration, from the Registration Honoris de Richmond, shows William the Conqueror granting lands to his nephew, the earl of Brittany. Though possibly a more elaborate ceremony that that which would have occurred in Ireland, the grant, the seal, the kneeling recipient and the men-at-arms would have been similar. (*The Popular History of England*, vol. 1, p. 194)
98. The Charter issued by Henry II to the city of Dublin in 1171–2 by which he gave Dublin to 'men of Bristol' – mentioned in the fourth line. (Dublin Corporation Archives)
99. The Rock of Cashel in Co Tipperary. (Irish Tourist Board)
100. Selskar Abbey, Co Wexford, founded for regular Canons by the Norse, was called the priory of St. Peter and St Paul

of Selskar; the Roche family were its patrons and bene-factors. The oldest part of the abbey, which would have been familiar to Henry II, is the part to the left; the square tower is a later addition. (F. Grose, *Antiquities*, vol. 2, p. 59)

101. Hugh de Lacy. He wears an orange-brown tunic, red hose and black shoes. (Ms 700: National Library of Ireland)

102. The so-called King John's Castle at Carlingford, Co Louth, had in fact nothing to do with the king. It was built by Hugh de Lacy to control the waterways. (F. Grose, *Antiquities*, vol. 2, p. 3)

103. When Hugh de Lacy was granted Meath, he made Trim his capital and it has always been accepted that he starting building Trim Castle, the impressive ruins of which still stand, in 1173. However when the Office of Public Works was doing some excavations recently for a restoration programme, it raised doubts as to whether Trim was the usual motte-and-bailey type and whether it may not date from the next century. Francis Grose says: 'In 1221, Earl Marshall had great conflicts with Hugh de Lacy; Meath was harassed between them, and Trim besieged; but it fortunately escaped being taken; and shortly after a new and much stronger castle was built on the ruins of the old one.' This would seem to bear out the later date. (F. Grose, *Antiquities*, vol. 2, facing p. 65)

104. The foundation charter of Dunbrody Abbey, Co Wexford, recites that Hervey de Monte Marisco, 'seneschal to Richard, earl of Pembroke, made a grant of divers lands to St Mary and St Benedict, and to the monks of the abbey of Blidewas in Shropshire, for erecting an abbey at Dunbrody for Cistercian monks.' It was badly damaged during the Rebellion of 1798 and the tomb of Hervey was destroyed. (F. Grose, *Antiquities*, vol. 1, facing p. 46)

105. Tintern Abbey. Grose relates: 'William, earl of Pembroke, being in great peril at sea, made a vow to found an abbey in that place where he should first land: this was at Tintern, where he settled a convent of Cistercians, and dedicated the building to the Virgin Mary. The monks he brought from Tintern Abbey in Monmouthshire, and gave them many parcels of land, and liberties, equal to those of the abbey of Dunbrody. (F. Grose, *Antiquities*, vol. 1, between pp. 50 and 51)

106. Dundrum Castle is north-east of the Mourne Mountains in

Co Down. Here John de Courcy built a motte-and-bailey castle *c.*1177 in an almost impregnable position. The castle was later enlarged and strengthened. (F. Grose, *Antiquities*, vol. 1, plate 1)

107. Probably the first true castle to be build in Ireland. Carrickfergus, Co Antrim, is traditionally assigned to John de Courcy, though Hugh de Lacy is also a possibility. Built between 1180 and 1205, it has a massive keep and high curtain walls. (Bartlett, *Scenery and Antiquities*, vol. 1, facing p. 2)

108. *Treasures from the National Library of Ireland* notes: 'The symbol of the crowns in triplicate served as the mark of the lordship of Ireland in late-medieval times and was probably inspired by the paperl tiara. In the manuscript the artist seems to be considering possible arrangements of the crowns.' (*A Treatise on Heraldry*, 1345, GO Ms 7, National Library of Ireland)

109. Castleknock is a good illustration of the motte-and-bailey type of fortification first built by the Normans. The land was given by Strongbow to Hugh Tirrel and the lordship of the Tirrels lasted for several centuries. Grose records an ancient tradition about Castleknock: 'There was a window at Castle Knock, neither glazed nor latticed, yet a candle being set there in the highest wind or storm burns as quiet as in a perfect calm.' (F. Grose, *Antiquities*, vol. 1, facing p. 8)

110. Seal of King John to Magna Charta (left), and reverse (right). (*The Popular History of England*, vol. 1, pp. 322, 344)

111. The priory of Athassel, one of the largest in Ireland, was founded *c.*1200 by William de Burgo for Augustinian Canons. Athassel was an immensely rich foundation – Ledwich refers to the 'taste of the Augustinians, seconded by the opulence of their patrons, which produced Graignemanagh, Monaincha and the Priory of Athassel'. Ledwich's *Antiquities*, facing p. 133)

112. Youghal Abbey was founded by Maurice FitzGerald the Second though it was largely rebuilt in the second half of the fifteenth century. Bartlett, *Scenery and Antiquities*, vol. 2, facing p. 89)

113. Kells, Co Kilkenny, was founded in 1193 by Geoffrey FitzRobert for Augustinian Canons he had brought over from Bodmin in Cornwell. Little remains from this period – the strongly fortified walls date from the fifteenth and

sixteenth centuries. They enclose an area of five acres, making Kells the largest monastic enclosure in Ireland. (The Office of Public Works)

114. Molana Abbey lies on an island in the Blackwater estuary in Co Waterford. Created for Augustinian Canons, it was built on the site of a sixth-century abbey. It is here that Raymond le Gros is buried. (Irish Tourist Board)

115. King John gave Limerick city a charter in 1197 and ordered the building of a strong castle to command the old Thomond bridge across the Shannon. It has massive corner towers and a twin-towered gate building. (Bartlett, *Scenery and Antiquities*, vol. 1, facing p. 107).

116. The family of Bermingham was early settled in Connaught, according to Grose, 'and were no mean assistants in aiding the English in subduing it. This castle (at Athenry) was constructed to secure his possessions by Pierce de Bermingham, in the reign of King John, by whom he was summoned to parliament and had a grant of 20 marks a year, payable out of the exchequer of Dublin for his support in the king's service.' (F. Grose, *Antiquities*, vol. 1, facing p. 65)

117. The Butler coat of arms: 1st and 4th, or a chief indented azure; 2nd and 3rd, Gules three covered cups or. (Terry Myler)

118. The Browne (de Brun) coat of arms: Or an eagle displayed with two heads sable. (Terry Myler)

119. The de Lacy coat of arms: Or a lion rampart purpure. (Terry Myler)

120. The Nugent coat of arms: Ermine two bars gules. (Terry Myler)

121. Francis Grose writes: 'On being appointed Lord Justice of Ireland in 1173, (Strongbow) laid the foundation of a castle in Kilkenny, but it was scarcely finished when it was demolished by the insurgent Irish. However, William Earl Marshal, descended from Strongbow, and also Lord Justice, in 1195, began a noble pile on a more extensive plan, and on the ancient site; a great part of this fine castle has survived the convulsions of this distracted kingdom and continues at this day a conspicuous ornament of the beautiful city of Kilkenny.' The castle eventually passed into the possession of the dukes of Ormond. The illustration is of a bastion tower. (F. Grose, *Antiquities*, vol. 1, facing p. 29)

122. Coat of arms of the Roche family: Gules three roaches naint in pale argent. Crest: On a rock proper an osprey rising argent beaked and legged or holding in the claws a roach argent. Motto: *'Mon Dieu est ma roche'*

123. The Halls, noting the disappearance of old town of Bannow beneath the sand, record: 'The church is obviously of very remote origin. The windows are not of the pointed Gothic, such as were introduced by the Normans; but Saxon, similar to those of Cormac's Chapel, and in the style of architecture known to have existed in Ireland long prior to the invasion. The interior is filled with sculptured ornaments of great beauty as well as antiquity; and the comparatively modern graves of the "lords of the soil" are mingled with those of their great English progenitors – for perhaps in no county of Ireland can there be found so many who trace their descent in a direct line from the triumphant knights of the reign of Henry the Second.'

The Halls also noted the abundance of sea-fowl in the bay, including the barnacle goose which Giraldus pronounced to be the product of the barnacle and therefore fish and not flesh – a dispensation greatly welcomed during the fast days of Lent, as it could be eaten. In the words of one learned man: 'Whatever is naturally born of flesh is flesh, but this bird had no such origin, therefore it is not flesh.' (Mr and Mrs. S. C. Hall, *Ireland: Its Scenery, Character etc*, London, 1841–43, vol. II, p. 153)

124. The promontory of Baginbun. (Halls' *Ireland*, vol. II, p. 146)

125. The Christ Church of the Vikings was founded *c*.1050 by Ragnvald, son of Sigtrygg. (*Reginald's Tower and the Story of Waterford*)

126. The penance of Henry II before Becket's shrine in Canterbury Cathedral. (From an ancient painting on glass)

127. One of the magnificent effigies in the ruined church at Hospital, Co Limerick (so called after the hospital founded there by the Knights Hospitallers in 1215). This is said to be that of its founder Geoffrey de Marisco. (Office of Public Works)

Select Bibliography

R. I. Best, Osborn Bergin and M.A. O'Brien (eds.), *The Book of Leinster* (Dublin, 1954)

F. S. Byrne, *Irish Kings and High-Kings* (London, 1973)

Edmund Curtis, *A History of Ireland* (London, 1936)

Edmund Curtis, *A History of Medieval Ireland from 1086 to 1513* (London, 1923)

William Camden, *Britannia* (London, 1695)

Michael Dolley, *Anglo-Norman Ireland, c. 1100–1318* (Dublin, 1972)

J. C. Davis, *Giraldus Cambrensis 1146–1946;* in *Archaeologia Cambrensis 99* (1946–7)

Thomas Forester (ed. T. Wright), *The Historical Works of Giraldus Cambrensis* (London, 1863)

W. H. Hennessy (ed.), *Annals of Loch Cé* (London, 1871)

W. H. Hennessy and B. MacCarthy (eds.), *Annals of Ulster* (Dublin, 1887–1901)

Richard Holinshed, *Chronicles* (London, 1587)

H. G. Leask, *Irish Castles and Castellated Houses* (Dundalk, 1941)

J. E. Lloyd, *History of Wales* (London, 1939)

S. MacAirt (ed.), *Annals of Inisfallen* (Dublin, 1951)

R. A. S. Macalister, *Lebor Gabála Éireann* (Irish Texts Society: London, 1939)

Eoin MacNeill, *Celtic Ireland* (Dublin and London, 1921)

F. X. Martin, *No Hero in the House: Diarmait MacMurchada and the Coming of the Normans to Ireland* (Dublin, 1977; O'Donnell lecture, 1975)

T. W. Moody and F. X. Martin (eds.), *The Course of Irish History* (Cork, 1984)

D. Murphy (ed.), *Annals of Clonmacnoise* (Dublin, 1896)

Ken Nicholls, *Gaelic and Gaelicised Ireland in the Middle Ages* (Dublin 1972)

Kate Norgate, 'The Bull "Laudabiliter" ' (*English Historical Review 8*: London, 1893)

Donncha Ó Corráin, *Ireland before the Normans* (Dublin, 1972)

J. F. O'Doherty, 'Rome and the Anglo-Irish Invasion of Ireland' (*Irish Ecclesiastical Record* 42; Dublin, 1933)

John O'Donovan (ed. and trans.) *Annals of the Kingdom of Ireland by the Four Masters* (Dublin, 1851)

John J. O'Meara, *The First Version of the Topography of Ireland* (Dundalk, 1951)

G. H. Orpen, *Ireland under the Normans, 1169–1333* (Oxford, 1911–20)

G. H. Orpen (ed. and trans.), *Song of Dermot and the Earl* (Oxford, 1892)

A. J. Otway-Ruthven, *A History of Medieval Ireland* (London, 1968)

Joseph Raftery (ed.), *The Celts* (Cork, 1964)

Alan Reid, *The Castles of Wales* (London, 1973)

John Ryan, *Irish Monasticism: Origins and Early Development* (Dublin, 1934)

A. B. Scott and F. X. Martin (eds.), *Expugnatio Hibernica: The Conquest of Ireland, by Giraldus Cambrensis* (Dublin, 1978)

Sir Frank Stenton (ed.), *The Bayeux Tapestry* (London, 1957)

Whitley Stokes (ed.), *Annals of Tighernach* (in *Revue Celtique*, 1895–7)

Thomas Wright (ed. and trans.), *Song of Dermot and the Earl* (London, 1837)

Acknowledgements

In the compiling of this book I found it necessary to quote from numerous other works. To the various authors, editors or publishers I am deeply grateful for permission to quote from the works listed here:

Ireland under the Normans by Goddard H. Orpen (Clarendon Press, Oxford); *The Historical Works of Giraldus Cambrensis* translated by Thomas Forester, MA, and revised and edited by Thomas Wright, MA, FSA (George Bell & Sons, London); *The Song of Dermot and the Earl* translated by Goddard H. Orpen (Clarendon Press, Oxford); *A History of Ireland* and *A History of Medieval Ireland* both by Edmund Curtis (Methuen, London); *The History of Ireland to the Coming of Henry II* by Arthur Ua Clerigh (Ernest Benn, London); *Social England* by Reginald Poole (Cassell, London); *Ireland and the Anglo-Norman Church* by G. T. Stokes, DD (Hodder & Stoughton, London); *Itinerary of Archbishop Baldwin through Wales, and Description of Wales* by Giraldus Cambrensis, translated by R. C. Hoare (Everyman's Library edition, J. M. Dent, London, and E. P. Dutton, New York; *England under the Angevin Kings* by Kate Norgate (Macmillan, London); *John of Salisbury* by C. C. Webb (Methuen, London); *Historical Portraits of Irish Chieftains and Anglo-Norman Knights* by Rev. Charles B. Gibson (Longmans Green, London); *History of Ireland* by Abbé James MacGeoghegan (James Duffy, Dublin); *The Geraldines* by Brian FitzGerald (Staples Press, London); *A Short History of the Irish People* by Mary Hayden and George A. Moonan (The Educational Company of Ireland, Dublin); *The Course of Irish History,* chapters on the Anglo-Norman invasion of Ireland, by Rev. Prof. F. X. Martin, OSA, and Ireland in the eleventh and twelfth centuries by Prof. Brian O Cuiv (The Mercier Press, Cork, for Radio Telefis Eireann); *Historical Criticism of The Song of Dermot and the Earl* by Rev. Prof. J. F. O'Doherty in *Irish Historical Studies,* Vol. I, No. 2, September 1938 (Hodges Figgis, Dublin); *Miscellaneous Irish*

Annals edited by Seamus O hInnse (Dublin Institute for Advanced Studies); *Journal of the Waterford and South-East Ireland Archaeological Society*, Vols. 1 and 5 (Royal Society of Antiquaries of Ireland, Dublin); *The Catholic Encyclopedia* (Caxton, London); *Rome and the Anglo-Norman Invasion of Ireland* by Rev. Prof. J. F. O'Doherty in *The Irish Ecclesiastical Record*, Vol. XLII (Browne & Nolan, Dublin); *The Lament for John Mac Walter Walsh* by J. C. Walsh (Kelmscott Press, New York); *The Origin and Development of Wexford Town* by Dr George W. Hadden in *The Journal of the Old Wexford Society*, No. 1, 1968.

I would also like to express thanks to the staffs of the National Library and the Central Catholic Library, Dubin; to Rev. Prof. F. X. Martin for advice and encouragement; to the late Charlie D. Hearne, former national teacher and recognised sage of Fethard, Co Wexford, for invaluable information on Baginbun and Bannow, and to many other friends and well wishers who loaned me books and manuscripts, provided advice and insights, and generally made the tasks of research and writing both enjoyable and rewarding.

The publishers and I are indebted to the following for their kind permission to use copyright photographic material: Cadw (Welsh Historic Monuments); Dublin Corporation Archives; Mary Evans Pictorial Picture Library; Flynn's Photo Service; the Irish Tourist Board; Lambeth Palace Library; the Office of Public Works; the National Library of Ireland; The National Museum of Ireland; Phaidon Press (for the Bayeux Tapestry references); The South East Regional Tourist Organisation; Trinity College Dublin.

The engravings are from those tireless travellers and recorders of the Irish scene over the past two centuries – W. H. Bartlett, Francis Grose and his nephew Daniel, Mr and Mrs Hall and Edward Ledwich.

Index

RICHARD ROCHE was born of farming stock in south Wexford where his Norman-Flemish ancestors first settled in the twelfth century. After brief spells as teacher and trawler-hand he took up journalism and served on provincial papers before reaching Dublin. He has worked on the *Evening Press,* the *Irish Times* and the *Irish Independent,* from which he took early retirement in 1986. He has contributed to many other papers and periodicals in Ireland and his work has appeared also in English, US, German, Portuguese and Spanish publications.

History, particularly local history, is one of his hobbies. A well-known lecturer and broadcaster, he is a Fellow of the Royal Society of Antiquaries of Ireland and the author of several books: *Here's Their Memory,* which dealt with County Wexford's part in the struggle for national independence since 1793; *Freedom the Wolfe Tone Way,* in which he collaborated with Sean Cronin in editing a selection of Wolfe Tone's writings; *Saltees – Island of Birds and Legends* (with Oscar Merne); *The Texas Connection: Tales of the Wexford Coast.*